GROUPS ALIVE—CHURCH ALIVE

GROUPS ALIVE— CHURCH ALIVE

THE EFFECTIVE USE OF SMALL GROUPS IN THE LOCAL CHURCH

By CLYDE REID

1817

HARPER & ROW, PUBLISHERS

NEW YORK, EVANSTON, AND LONDON

LIBRARY OF CONGRESS CATALOG CARD NUMBER: 69-17008

69707172738765432

Dedicated to the members of two small groups which have been very significant in my life and my family's life—our neighborhood group in Grace Congregational Church, New York City, and our couples' group, the Congregational Church of Birmingham, Michigan

FOREWORD

The intensive group experience has been said to be, perhaps, the most significant social invention of this century. Certainly Carl Rogers is right in calling it one of the most rapidly growing social phenomena in our nation. Small groups have "exploded" into every part of our social order—institutional and organizational, corporate, educational, and religious. At the same time, they have "imploded" upon themselves by achieving new depths and intensities of interpersonal relationships, supported by a rapidly growing body of theoretical literature and experimental data.

At the present moment, however, much of this advance in theory and in effective practice remains with the experts. They produce and read the theoretical literature with its inevitable esoteric jargon; they carry on the experiments; and they move on to the next hypothesis before proven gains can be consolidated. The amateur, the ordinary individual seeking a productive and satisfying group experience, often is left to his own intuitions and unexamined behavior. In spite of the proliferation of training centers and programs, of books, symposia, and journals in the field, he is likely to find little help in terms he can afford or in language he can understand. The explosion spreads a flood of groups; the implosion compresses theory and experiment. He stands in the vacuum left between.

To this need of the seeking amateur, Dr. Reid's book will come as welcome succor and resource. Written out of a background fully conversant with theory and advanced practice, the book is scaled to the interest and competence of the ordinary group member. It gives him essential ideas that can be applied to what goes on in groups, and illustrates these by cases and instances with which the reader can easily identify his own experience. It offers guidance that is clear and relevant without making group life appear facile or superficial—the trap into which much popular literature in the field manages to fall. Moreover, Dr. Reid presents this material in a manner demonstrative of the authentic function of a group leader or a group member: by talking about his own group experiences—his feelings, frustrations, and gratifications as he has tried to help people enter into effective and satisfying group life. And most of all, he opens to the reader the reassurance that genuine group participation can bring that release of the self, the fulfillment of interpersonal relationships, and the joy of life together, which have become the primary longing of multitudes of persons in our time.

JOHN L. CASTEEL

CONTENTS

PREFACE

I am writing this book because I must. I have seen the lives of people change in small groups. I have seen people reborn in small groups. This is not using the word loosely, for individuals have gained a whole new foothold on life. My own life has been deeply affected and positively influenced by small groups, and my wife would tell you the same. I have seen people gain exciting new insights, I have seen them grow in self-confidence and self-acceptance, and I have seen persons come to know who they really are for the first time in their lives.

I am not here speaking of therapy groups, although the same claims would apply to them. I am speaking of a variety of small groups of relatively healthy people organized for various reasons. I am speaking of small groups which may be found in the life of any church, or which may exist around the edges of a church's life. It is my conviction that the average church anywhere can be greatly strengthened by the proper use of the power of the small group. Individuals can find deeper satisfaction in their church life, and the institution itself can more effectively achieve its stated goals, if careful attention is paid to the information in this book.

There are a number of fine books on the market which describe the exciting ways in which churches have utilized small groups to enrich the lives of people. However, this book is written primarily for those who work with small groups, who are interested in

11

working with small groups, or who want to understand their group better. The purpose is to set forth the important basic elements of group life. These are the factors in the life of a group which determine whether the group lives or dies, becomes productive and therapeutic or aborts into a useless, lifeless obligation. One of the most exciting and creative branches of social science today is the field of group psychology. The insights coming from that field ought to be available to those of us in the churches who work constantly with small groups, dead or alive. It is for this reason that I am bringing together some of these crucial insights, tested by my own long experience with group work.

I owe a debt of appreciation to many people for my own pilgrimage in this field. Dr. Walter Holcomb at Boston University first introduced me to the study of small groups, and the power of that initial experience led me to seek further opportunities. The Boston University Human Relations Center, and particularly Dr. Kenneth Benne and Dr. Warren Bennis, were deeply influential in guiding my early group experience, and I will always be grateful to these two men who have helped pioneer the emergence of a new science. Another early inspiration to me was the work being done by Dr. Gerald J. Jud at Central Congregational Church in Worcester, Massachusetts. Jerry's willingness to share his experience helped me see the practical possibilities of applying group insights in a local church. Dr. John L. Casteel offered me my first opportunity to work extensively with small groups of students at Union Theological Seminary in New York, and has continued to encourage me to share my insights and expand my horizons. The National Training Laboratories (now the NTL Institute for Applied Behavioral Science) likewise offered me an opportunity to grow personally and to work as a colleague with group trainers in a variety of settings.

Dr. Simon Doniger, editor of *Pastoral Psychology,* has long been a source of support and encouragement by publishing a number of my papers on small groups and inviting me to edit a special issue of that journal on "Ministry through Small Groups." Dr. Seward Hiltner, who conceived the idea for that special issue, has also encouraged me in many ways.

I must also express my appreciation to my colleagues at the

Institute for Advanced Pastoral Studies, where the small group is an integral part of the educational work carried on there. Dr. Reuel L. Howe has long recognized the importance of the small group as a crucible in which men test new insights, wrestle with communication blocks within themselves, and try new behavior. He has provided both support and freedom for me to work creatively with groups and to try new methods of making that work more effective. My colleagues, James P. Simmons and John J. Ziegler, Jr., have both taught me much and provided me with encouragement to experiment. Jim, in particular, has stimulated me to an awareness of the importance of the new thrust in non-verbal methods of communication.

In the preparation of this book, I was blessed with three charming assistants. Mrs. Nancy Mestrovic was most helpful and supportive as she typed the manuscript, and my secretary, Mrs. Patricia Hyatt, did an equally fine job on the revision. My wife, Bonnie (that's really her name), again provided invaluable help with her suggestions and her hours of proof-reading.

CLYDE REID

Bloomfield Hills, Michigan
February, 1969

_____

CHAPTER I

THE SMALL GROUP EXPLOSION

Jeff leaned forward in his chair, looking at the other group members intently. "The chapter we read this week made me realize that I wanted to share something with the group. Sharon and I have been having a rough time lately, and . . . well . . . I guess we just need your support while we're going through it." Sharon, sitting across the room, put her face down in her hands. The other four couples sat with serious faces, quietly waiting to see if Jeff wanted to say any more. "If it's support you need, you have that, Jeff," said Tom, putting a hand on Jeff's shoulder. Marilyn had slipped an arm around Sharon to comfort her.

"I've been under a lot of pressure at work lately, and I'm afraid I take it out on my family when I get home. I've been pretty grouchy with the kids, and I just haven't been very pleasant to live with, I guess."

Sharon looked up and interrupted, "Jeff, why didn't you talk to me about the pressure at the office? I'm not a mind reader. I felt that everything I did was unacceptable to you. I was beginning to doubt that you cared about me anymore." Jeff seemed surprised.

"I had been hoping for a promotion when Old John retired, but they brought in a new man instead." He spoke with some bitterness. "Then they had the gall to ask me to break him in. I thought they gave me a pretty rotten deal!"

Sharon moved over and sat beside her husband. "I wish you had told me. I could have shared some of the pain. This way you only drove me away and made things worse." She took his hand, and they hugged warmly. Everyone felt better.

Tom spoke up. "Jeff, I'm glad you could share that with us tonight."

"Well, I trust this group, and several of you have been willing to admit that you weren't perfect. It didn't seem to make you any weaker in my estimation, so I decided I could do the same."

This excerpt from the life of a small group is a symbol of our times. Small groups of every variety have sprung up in recent years, from prayer groups to personal growth groups. The couples' sharing group described above is another example. We are in the midst of an explosion of small groups of every imaginable sort. In the fields of criminology, mental health, social work, management and adult education, small groups are increasingly utilized, to name but a few. And the churches have not been exempt from this explosion of interest in the small group. Churches and church agencies everywhere are making use of small groups in exciting ways to bring new life and vitality into their midst.

Why is this so? Why is the small group becoming so important in so many fields of endeavor? I am convinced that one key reason is the deep hunger that exists in modern society. People everywhere are hungry for depth relationships. They need such relationships to give them a point of security and belonging in a world of rapid change and mass society. Small groups also can supply the deep needs of human beings for love and acceptance that are so impossible to find in a crowd of a hundred or a thousand. I like the way Elton Trueblood put it some years ago: "There is a vast amount of loneliness, and a consequent desire to belong to something. . . . Real fellowship is so rare and so precious that it is like dynamite in any human situation. Any group that will find a way to the actual sharing of human lives will make a difference either for good or ill in the modern world. . . ."[1]

I walked into a meeting the other day and ran into Marilyn

[1] *The Predicament of Modern Man* (New York: Harper & Row, 1944), pp. 100–101.

Smith, a lady I had known from a recent experience in a small group. She looked different, and I tried to figure out why. Slowly I realized that Marilyn had an exciting new hairdo. She also held herself more erect, as though proud to be a woman. She seemed dressed more attractively, and her face seemed more sparkling and alive. When I asked about the hairdo, she said that many things were new for her. An insight which emerged from the group experience had virtually changed her life.

We human beings are increasingly aware of our tremendous potential for growth and our ability to relate to others in depth. There is great power latent in a small group, and most of us have been exposed to demonstrations of that power. A friend recently returned from a week-long conference on the creative arts. She had enjoyed the week, but she was also feeling very frustrated. Sixty persons had attended the conference, and many sessions were spent in a large room where all sixty gathered for discussion. My friend was angry because she knew from experience that the group of sixty could have been divided to advantage. In smaller groups, each person would have had an opportunity to share his feelings and reactions, and the group members could have come to know each other in some depth. Like many people in our society today, she had experienced the value of small groups, and she felt frustrated and disappointed to be cheated of that enriching opportunity.

We are in the midst of an explosion of interest in the use of the small group. It has tremendous potentiality for the renewal of the church, as well as the enrichment of many other institutions in our culture. All church leaders, lay and clergy, who are concerned for more effective and exciting church life should examine the new insights on the subject with great seriousness.

THE USES OF SMALL GROUPS

Small groups are already being used within the life of our churches in a great variety of ways. The insights discussed in this book may be important and useful to persons working with them. I shall mention only a few of the more prominent methods now in use.

a. *Small groups are being used for educational purposes.* At the

Institute for Advanced Pastoral Studies, a center for the continuing education of church leaders, small groups have been used for years as a key element in the educational program. In his seminar group, Ken shares his personal anxiety about the changing role of the minister today. The group then discusses the positive as well as the problematic dimensions of that role, while helping Ken to understand his own difficulty in his ministry. While examining an important topic of common interest, they are also dealing with a crucial life issue for Ken—whether to stay in the ministry or not. If Ken feels affirmed by the group's response to his concern and their actual ministry to him, he may revise his feelings about his role.

At another point, Marvin may confess that Ken makes him angry and he feels he cannot trust Ken. So Marv disagrees with Ken on almost every issue that arises, and Ken feels equally antagonistic to Marv. The two men are helped to stand eyeball to eyeball and come to grips with their problem of communication. "You remind me of my minister at home who never listens to what I say," admits Marv, a teacher. And Ken counters, "You've been acting like my big brother who never did accept me." So learning in a small group can be immediate and deeply personal even while grounded in a solid academic framework.

Small groups are used educationally in church school classes and adult education programs as well. I know of several churches which are using intensive weekend retreats or workshops for a specific purpose such as developing stronger church leaders or training church school teachers. In such cases, the leaders often divide the group into small units of eight or ten persons to provide opportunity for deeper involvement and greater learning. Even the traditional church school class for adults is often divided into small discussion units where people get to know each other by first names. The old image of fifty elderly ladies nodding in their pews while someone presents a "Bible lecture" is vanishing at last, like the buffalo.

b. Small-group insights are enriching ongoing boards and committees. In many places, church leaders are utilizing boards and committees for more than church business. They are becoming aware that a trustees' meeting may provide an important occasion for the sharing of personal concerns and discussing key questions of faith. They are discovering that a meeting of deacons may be an opportunity for personal religious growth as well as a time to argue about who will slice up the bread into communion tidbits for next Sunday or whose turn it is to wash and iron the linen.

Picture a meeting of the Board of Trustees at Old First Church. Dr. Foming Wetmouth, minister of the church, is in a fine froth over the state of his parsonage roof. He tells the trustees how derelict they have been in their duty, harangues them about their Christian conscience, and personally appoints a subcommittee to check on the repairs of the roof. He cannot understand it when, a month later, the committee has not found time to get together. The dynamics of anger, resentment, and domination by Dr. Wetmouth are not understood by any of the group, perhaps, but the work does not get done.

When this minister and his board learn how to become an honest, sharing group, the board members should be able to tell Dr. Wetmouth why he makes them angry. Rather than sitting on their resentment of him, they should be able to share it with him in an adult way. On his side, he should be able to listen to their feelings and understand them better. When honesty and trust emerge, and when the members of a board know each other as caring persons, the work is likely to get done as well. This is not an easy task, but is well worth the pain involved if a deeper sense of community results.

c. Small groups are valuable for Bible-study, prayer, and discussion. I remember well the evening I spent visiting a Bible study group in Lexington, Massachusetts. The meeting was held in a church member's home, and no clergy were present. One member stood up and made an excellent summary presentation of his study of the passage assigned for the evening. Others added their insights from reading the passage, and open discussion followed. About fifteen persons were present, and most of them attended the twice monthly meetings in spite of their busy work schedules. I discovered a high level of interest and involvement in the group's discussion. This group was one of eighteen Bible study groups in the same church.

Some years before, a young couple, the Albert Wilsons, had gone to their pastor and indicated their interest in a study group. They did not feel that the usual Sunday morning program satisfied their deeper personal hunger for religious study. The pastor was wise. He offered to help them get started, but he would not lead the group himself. The group began with revolving lay leadership, and the minister soon pulled out. Thrown upon their own resources, the group flourished and later expanded into several groups, eventually into a parish-wide program with a deep influence on the life of that congregation.

Such study groups are not uncommon. I found a wide variety of Bible study groups, prayer groups, and discussion groups in a cross section of New England churches I studied a few years ago. They varied greatly in their organization and effectiveness. Some were highly centered in the minister as the teacher or lecturer. Others stressed the resources of the laymen and operated without clergy present, as the Lexington church groups. Some were quite formal with well-organized study requirements, while others were open, informal discussion groups of a personal nature. The important common element was their existence as small units in which people could be known by their first names and in which they could talk as well as listen. Some combined study with a period of silence or prayer for others. Some were focused on prayer, readings, and silence as the primary exercise of the group. Most met in the evenings, and were well attended by both men and women.

d. Small groups can lead to action in the world. My wife and I belonged to an interracial small group in New York City for most of the seven years we lived there. It was organized as a neighborhood unit of our local congregation. At various times that group was relatively inactive. At other times, it was the focal point for a variety of actions. It served variously as a reading and discussion group, a group for the sharing of personal concerns and the hammering out of convictions on such things as the new morality, a place for celebrating some joyful event in a member's life, and, on occasion, for the promotion of social concerns. I remember well the joy our group shared with us on the birth of our second child, and I remember their kindness when we moved to another city to establish our home. We shared happy moments, but we also organized civil rights rallies and spearheaded the establishment of a housing "clinic" in mid-Harlem. A great variety of activities expressed the life of that group, yet an outsider at some moments in its life could easily describe it as a self-centered group. There are times when groups, like individuals, need to be concerned with themselves. My family found that group supplying many of the fellowship, educational, and social reinforcement functions which a larger congregation often cannot provide. It was a very important aspect of our life in a large, impersonal city. We often found ourselves changing personal plans so that we would not have to miss a meeting of the group. Its members remain important persons to us.

It is certainly possible that small groups can become too centered upon trivia—too much concerned with the minor details of its members' lives and too little concerned for the world. However, the group which becomes mature *can* be concerned for both the lives of its members and the great social issues in the world around it. Furthermore, there is present in every small group the dynamic to do something significant about the social ills it confronts.

A final word needs to be added. The social concern of a small group may also be legitimately expressed in its ministry to needy persons in its midst. I shall never forget a visit to such a group in which several elderly persons were active. One retired lady told me confidentially after the meeting that she had recently been hospitalized for six weeks. She said, "This group has done more for me than any church has ever done, and I've been a church member all my life." The group had rallied around her, visited her, brought her flowers. In short, they had loved her. And I shall never forget a pathetic contrast to her story. I was speaking to the men's club in a large city church about the value of small groups. An elderly man stood up in the back of the room and cried, "Why, we don't need any such thing in this church! I was in the hospital for six months this year, and I want you to know I twice received a personally signed card from our minister. Not only that, but the men's club even sent me flowers!" For a human being to be content with so little of the milk of human kindness speaks of a lifelong starvation.

Small groups can be self-centered and dead. There are also excellent chances that they can be concerned for others, vital, and genuinely involved in the world. There are reasons why some groups are dead and others alive! The science of group psychology —group dynamics, as it is sometimes called—can help us to promote healthy groups in place of immature, self-centered ones. In fact, a study of these same group dynamics can help action-oriented groups become more effective in carrying out their tasks as well. The remaining chapters in this book will be calling attention to the important insights that can help us promote mature, concerned small groups.

  e. *Small groups enrich seasonal worship programs.* How often have you opened your mail in the spring to find a little folder which reads something like this: "We know you will want to attend the special series of Lenten meetings on Thursday evenings at the church. On Thursday, March 1, the Reverend Drury Speaker will preach on 'Churching the Unchurched.' On Thursday, March 8, the Reverend Ernest Christian will deliver the message on 'Unchurching the Churched.' Etc. We know you will not want to miss this outstanding series of stimulating Lenten messages." Ha, ha ha! It has been my experience that when church people are honest, they will admit that they are weary to death of attending a series of Lenten worship services. They are tired of adding one more boring repetition of the Sunday service, with some "outside" speaker delivering the sermon in place of the regular minister. Even if the choir does sing. Even if a common theme unites the series of speeches! Even if there is a special "congregational sing" preceding the pastoral prayer!

  Many churches have found Lent or Advent an excellent time to involve the members of the congregation in an opportunity to express themselves. By arranging a series of small discussion meetings in members' homes, they involve a large number of persons in a meaningful educational activity without boring them to death. There are many ways in which such meetings may be structured. The sermon from the previous Sunday may be mimeographed and studied for discussion at evening meetings later in the week. An important current theme that has been concerning the congregation may be established for each week. Small groups with a clear focus of concern can enrich a short-term study program in this way. It is advisable to train a group of discussion leaders in some of the skills of discussion leading. If one member moderates each group to assure that each person has an opportunity to speak, it can enhance the experience for everyone. On occasion, a neighborhood meeting of this sort catches fire, and the members do not want to give up the group.

f. Small groups improve communication through preaching. A church in Japan has become known for its unusual worship services. Following a brief sermon, members of the congregation divide up into small units and meet in various parts of the building to discuss the message. They then return to the sanctuary for the conclusion of the service. A church in Connecticut found that many of its members were away on weekends during the summer. They instituted a Wednesday evening service at which the minister preached a ten-minute sermon. This was followed by discussion and conversation, after which the minister concluded the worship service. Coffee and cookies were served during the discussion period.

Churches have experimented with a variety of programs like these in which the sermon is discussed. In some instances, the group meets during the week before the sermon is preached. This gives them an opportunity to wrestle with the preacher's theme and contribute to it from their experience and reflection. In other designs, the groups meet following the morning service or as an element of the service. Some preachers meet with the group, while others prefer to leave it free of clerical influence. Some ministers listen to a tape recording of the discussion later.

If we are earnest about wanting people to take our sermons seriously, then modern communication research points out that we must establish some method of feedback.[2] To establish such a two-way flow of communication between preacher and listeners, we must find methods which allow the layman to talk back. If he has no opportunity to express himself on the theme of the sermon, his interest and involvement will be distinctly lower. If he is allowed this opportunity, his interest in the preaching will be higher

---

[2] Dr. Reuel L. Howe has discussed a commonly used method of sermon discussion in his book, *Partners in Preaching* (New York: Seabury Press, 1968). My book *The Empty Pulpit* also outlines some models for sermon feedback (New York: Harper & Row, 1967).

and his involvement in the life of the church will also be deeper.

In *The Empty Pulpit* I have discussed the problem of preaching and communication, and have outlined a number of methods of sermon discussion. My research, reported in that book in some detail, indicates that small group discussion clearly increases the listener's sensitivity to preaching.

g. Small groups may focus on personal growth. A pastor I know discovered that many of his parishioners were hungry for a creative group experience. After much thought, he sent a letter inviting any persons interested in a group where they could come together regularly to seek, to ask and answer some of life's deepest questions, to meet at the parsonage on Sunday night. He pointed out that the purpose of such a group would be "nothing less than a complete reorientation to all of life." He also indicated that it was his hope that in the group they would come to experience God's power and presence and find a new commitment to Jesus Christ. That first Sunday night, forty-five persons showed up at the parsonage. (Another man I know issued such an invitation and one person showed up—so they began there.) Of those forty-five, thirty-six committed themselves to a weekly group meeting for one year. The keynote of their meetings is openness and freedom in which persons can share anything they have on their minds and be truly themselves. In the minister's words, "We are not trying to impress each other, but rather to accept and love each other as we are, simply because we are persons, children of God. In this sense, we minister to each other in the deepest ways."[3]

Many churches now offer opportunities to belong to small sharing groups, in which members learn to listen to one another and share one another's burdens. It is advisable to have a trained leader for groups which have personal growth as their primary focus. This will be a minister or other person with some psychological background and some clinical experience, who feels comfortable in handling strong emotions, both anger and tenderness. Increasingly, ministers are being trained in psychological sensitivity as well as theological understanding. Through clinical train-

[3] Otis E. Young, "A Reorientation to All of Life," *Pastoral Psychology*, March, 1967.

ing programs in hospitals and more sensitive seminary preparation, they are entering their work with more ability to work with people. Too often in the past they have received a fine classical education in theological ideas, but little training in how to work with people. As a result the minister's ideas, fine as they may be, remain *his* ideas. His inability to relate to people prevents them from accepting and identifying with his insights.

We are increasingly aware that theology is of no avail unless it brings together or correlates actions and ideas. The minister who preaches love, yet cannot express warmth to his people, is really communicating a contradiction. The meaning he conveys is an intellectualized, sterile kind of love, and his people will probably be baffled by his inability to live his message. And we have all known church members who say to us: "I have been saved, and I now belong to the fellowship of loving, forgiving persons who follow Jesus Christ. I want you to be saved, too, or you are not really acceptable to me." He, too, communicates a contradiction. For this reason it is important to have a group in which we can face who we are and find a loving, accepting community to help us improve our personal relationships. This is but one of the exciting new frontiers open to the community we call the church, as that institution seeks new styles of life for a new day.

h. Some churches organize into mission groups. The typical organization of the Protestant church into deacons and deaconesses, trustees, social concerns committee, religious education committee, and men's and women's organizations leaves much to be desired. This arrangement usually has about as much life in it as an old turtle shell—minus the turtle. When it moved, it was slow at best. Without the organism that once inhabited it, this structure has very little dynamic left, yet remains hard to crack open.

The organization of the Church of the Saviour in Washington, D.C., is a refreshing contrast. The basic unit of the church's life is the small mission group. Each group carries out a task in the world or in the church, a task they have grown to feel it is their calling to fulfill. The shape of the task changes, but the groups are also structured so as to be sensitive to the need for constant reevaluation and change. Each member of this unusual church finds his place in one of these mission groups, so the congregation holds no mere spectators. Each member is actively involved and deeply known as a person, with a first name and with real concerns, through his relationship to the mission group. Elizabeth O'Connor has described the recent work of the Church of the Saviour in her book, *Journey Inward, Journey Outward*.[4] Mission groups are involved with such diverse projects as renovating housing in the inner city and maintaining the church's coffee house, The Potter's House.

This division of a church into small functioning units with a relatively focused task demonstrates an important principle of human nature. People like to be involved in worthwhile ventures which challenge them, call out their gifts, *and allow them the opportunity to be involved in the decisions* that shape the task. They will give generously of their time, energy, and money if they are really convinced that the task is important and worth doing. Similarly, people are weary of holding up the empty turtle shell, of doing a lot of "mickey-mouse" jobs that don't really matter. I know many people who have lost interest in their churches because they have never been asked to do anything but arrange the flowers on the altar, usher once a month, or serve coffee at a church supper.

I know of a social action committee in a suburban church which met monthly. People often came late or failed to show up. The meetings consisted of intellectual discussions about social action projects. Individually, some of the members of the committee were deeply involved in action programs. However, when this group began holding sessions with a similar group from an inner-city ghetto church, the committee meetings came alive. Attendance and interest went up.

Sitting on a committee which verbally reviews the same tired program and voices the same pet peeves every month does not excite the imagination or command the loyalty of very many people today. It is little wonder that they do not come on time—if at all—to many church boards and committees. One live alternative to this problem of boredom and low morale is to structure the

<hr />

[4] New York: Harper & Row, 1968.

congregation into smaller units who talk, sweat, pray, and act together to carry out their mission in the world.

i. Small groups are used for therapeutic purposes. "My therapy group has been terribly important to me. I've been able to discover who I am really for the first time in my life. I now have greater confidence in myself, because the group helped me to understand that I am acceptable. I never knew that before." This statement could have been made by any number of persons I have known, for therapy groups have been flourishing in recent years. Psychiatrists and psychologists find that group therapy has advantages over individual therapy for some patients. Similarly, some ministers trained in pastoral counseling have turned to group counseling as a new and exciting healing method.

One minister I know recently began a group for persons in his church who found themselves at some kind of crossroads or crisis point in life. A psychologist works with the minister as a consultant to this group. Another minister leads a series of group sessions each year on death, bereavement, and grief, an area in which most of us need insight.

The group approach has some clear advantages. One of these lies in the simple arithmetic of time. A trained group counselor can help more people with the same investment of time by bringing them together in small groups. However, the value of the group approach is far greater than the fact that it is a time-saving device. In a small group, the person in need finds persons in his group who represent for him a mother, or father, or someone else who has been particularly difficult for him to get along with. In the group, and with the group's help, he is often able to work out some of these problems of relationship. Furthermore, the group provides a supportive context, a place where he is known in depth, yet loved and accepted by persons who also have personal difficulties.

While it cannot be stressed too firmly that untrained persons should not try to lead therapy groups or counseling groups, it is also true that those who want to enrich their counseling ministry may profit by seeking training in this specialty.[5]

[5] For a fuller treatment of this theme, see Joseph W. Knowles, *Group Counseling* (Englewood Cliffs, N.J.: Prentice-Hall, 1964).

It is also a fact that there are often therapeutic effects for persons who are members of small groups of many types. The loving, accepting fellowship of a group of persons who really know each other can help us to face ourselves more realistically. A group can also provide strength for the facing of personal crises and insight into problems of relationship that so often plague and bind us. We are often enabled to accept ourselves when we discover that we are acceptable to others. The Alcoholics Anonymous organization utilizes this power of the group to help individuals find the support necessary to break the alcohol habit. There are therapeutic effects which emerge from membership in such a group, although the group is not organized as a therapy group. There is now an organization similar to Alcoholics Anonymous for persons who have had professional therapy. In these groups, former patients support each other with insight and acceptance, often helping the individual to keep his balance in life.

SOME BASIC CONVICTIONS

In summary, this book rests upon four basic convictions and one major premise. The convictions are as follows:

1. *The average pastor in the average church can do much to enhance the ministry of that church if he sees the leadership of small groups as an important part of his role.* Many ministers today have had no training in such leadership, yet work with small groups nearly every day of the week. The emerging science of group psychology has a rich deposit of insights and resources to offer him. Increasingly, our trained leadership should be helped to use this resource to further the work of the church.

I received my introduction to group training in a seminary course followed by clinical pastoral training and a human relations laboratory experience. There are today many opportunities for church leaders to receive small group training, and there is no substitute for a training experience. Reading about small groups simply does not educate one as actual involvement does. Many universities and theological schools now offer group experiences,

---

[6] Some helpful addresses are listed in the back of the book on page 125.

and local counseling centers and mental health facilities provide such help. The NTL Institute for Applied Behavioral Science in Washington, D.C., continues to offer workshops in Bethel, Maine, and in other centers around the country.[6] This is the group which pioneered with their programs in group dynamics, and people come from around the world to attend their workshops. The Institute for Advanced Pastoral Studies also offers training in small group leadership.

2. *There are some dynamic processes common to groups of all kinds which can be identified to great advantage by any group leader.* Whenever we bring human beings together in a situation where they can become involved with each other, there are some basic interactions that tend to emerge. Every group must establish a leadership pattern, for example. We can ignore that leadership pattern or we can be sensitive to it. In the following chapters, I shall spell out some of these basic dynamic processes. Group leaders may profit by being aware of these dimensions of group life.

3. *Small groups have tremendous potential for releasing the real ministry of the church.* The creative uses of small groups in the life of the church are many. They can be structured to help youth encounter each other and their faith more profoundly. They can provide the context for a meeting between youth and adults that can help bridge the generation gap. Groups can bring persons into deep communication across the racial and class barriers which seem so impenetrable at times. They can help persons discover themselves and their identity.

It is this tremendous potential, this exciting dimension of the possible, that has led me to pursue my investigation into the frontier of small group research. Largely because of the unlimited possibilities offered by this avenue, I have come to have new hope for what can happen in the churches if we take small groups seriously.

4. *The possibility of shared leadership in groups, used experimentally in some human relations training situations, may offer great promise for the future of the church.* I read recently in the newspaper that one major religious group has experienced a decline of 75 per cent in the number of persons entering the ordained

ministry in the last few years. There appears to be a general decline of interest in the ministry as a profession. At the same time, there are many churches which cannot afford a full-time, highly educated clergyman. The possibility now exists that we may learn how to release the leadership potential in a small group of ordinary persons by providing appropriate help in getting them started. The concept of shared leadership, in which the group does not remain dependent upon the established leader, may open all kinds of possibilities to the small, struggling church. This power to release the potential locked up in a group may be the most important contribution of this new science to the life of the churches.

I have said that this book also rests upon a major premise. This is closely related to point four, above, and may be simply stated: *It is the task of the group leader in most instances to free the group from emotional dependence upon him, allowing it to emerge into a style of life in which each member shares responsibility for the life of the group.* This premise will be dealt with at some length in the chapter on group leadership, but will underlie much of the discussion that follows.

I should also like to share a vision and a hope. I have a vision of churches renewed and revitalized, more alive to the present, more involved with the real needs of people. I see churches in which people are not ashamed to know each other, nor to love each other, nor to share each other's burdens. I see churches in which there is a deeper inner life through a variety of small groups; and because of that vital inner life, a genuine reaching out to the world—a "journey inward, journey outward."

These are groups in which persons find themselves accepted fully and loved for who they are, with all their shortcomings. These are groups which inspire and encourage and support us in our personal crises, so that we do not bear them by ourselves and sit lonely in our pews on Sunday morning crying silently inside. These are groups which speak to our deepest needs to be reconciled to our wives and husbands, to communicate with our youth, to know our God, and to triumph over life. This is the deeper meaning of the ministry of pastoral care and the involvement of the laity in that ministry.

This is not just a utopian vision. I have hope for this vision, because I have seen the signs of it alive here and there. It will mean the constant retraining of our leadership—our whole leadership, lay and clergy. It will be a mammoth task, but then the Christian Church has faced mammoth tasks before.

CHAPTER II

ESTABLISHING THE CONTRACT

BILL: It's getting late and we need to get home pretty soon. We told our baby-sitter ten-thirty.

MARILYN: Yes, we should be starting home too.

PAUL: What are we going to do next time?

JUNE: I thought of a book the group might be interested in reading.

JENNY: When is our next meeting? We're going to be out of town two weeks from tonight. Could we meet on Thursday next time?

ED: I have a meeting on Thursdays. How about three weeks from tonight?

JEAN: What book did you have in mind, June?

RICH: We really must start. Our sitter is only an eighth-grader. . . . Let us know what you decide. Come on, Jenny.

JUNE: Oh, let me get your coats! I'm sorry you have to leave. We were really just getting started.

BILL: Are we going to close with silence again tonight?

Problem: Many groups never establish their basic contract on major aspects of the group's life. Persons come to meetings with differing expectations and often leave disappointed and frustrated when those expectations are not met.

The excerpt from the life of a typical group reported above probably sounds familiar. Many groups flounder or fail because some of the crucial decisions necessary to creative functioning are not made and clearly agreed upon. Group members may go home with vastly different ideas about what the group has agreed to do. The primary task of any new group is to make some important basic decisions and put them down in black and white in order to keep misunderstandings at a minimum. This process of making basic decisions about the life of the group may be thought of as the *group contract*.

The idea of a contract has emerged from the field of psychotherapy. When a man comes to a professional counselor or psychiatrist, or to his minister, he is often in a state of distress. One of the counselor's jobs is to listen, and then propose some kind of contract to his client. He may suggest that the man come to see him again the following week for further evaluation of the problem. He is thereby limiting the contract to one additional forty-five-minute meeting and outlining the basic content of the session, namely, further discussion of the client's problem.

At the end of the second meeting, the counselor may propose another contract. He may suggest that he and his client establish a regular meeting each week or twice a week for several months to dig in on a particular issue which seems to be at the heart of the matter. Or he may suggest that his client really needs to come once more and bring his wife with him. He may propose any number of alternatives.

The contract may also include discussion of fees—how much is to be paid, and when. It usually includes the basic elements necessary to continue the relationship, with sufficient definition of what, when, where, and why it is being continued. The counselor should define what he is equipped to do for the client and what he expects of him. When such a contract is agreed upon and clearly understood, the time spent together is more likely to be used to the advantage of both parties. The idea of contract may be equally important in a marriage, where the partners may have conflicting ideas of what the other partner has agreed to do and be.

It is my belief that every group should establish a clear contract early in its life. There are six elements of group life which seem important to clarify early as part of the contract if a group is to function efficiently.

1. The *purpose* for the group's meeting should be commonly understood. I recall an occasion when my wife referred to something that had gone on in "our prayer group."

"What prayer group?" I said.

"You know, *our group* that meets on Friday nights."

"Oh," I replied, "I hadn't thought of it as a prayer group." It was true that the group in question spent some time in silent meditation, but our meetings also had included discussion of a book and personal sharing. It had never occurred to me to think of it primarily as a prayer group. My wife and I had somewhat different contracts in mind in relation to that group and its primary purpose.

Every group needs a clear agreement on the purpose or purposes for which its members are gathering. If group members come with differing expectations, they are only inviting frustration and conflict when some of these expectations are disappointed. I recall a series of Lenten meetings a friend once attended. The two ministers on the staff of the church took turns leading the meetings. Minister A would speak briefly, then allow the individuals present to share their feelings freely. My friend found this very satisfying. Minister B talked at much greater length, leaving very little opportunity for the group to say anything. She found this very frustrating. She had a particular contract in mind, which included her right to speak and test her ideas with the group. Her contract agreed with that of Minister A, while Minister B offered a different one. If the contract had been clarified with the group at the beginning, and they had understood that Minister B's pattern would be the accepted procedure, the frustration probably would not have arisen. Or if Minister A and Minister B had worked out a common pattern, even a compromise of some sort, the group would have been more willing to live with the contract. When expectations and reality do not meet, unnecessary frustration may block the progress of the group.

So someone needs to decide whether the group is meeting for the purpose of hearing a lecture, engaging in open discussion, hearing a short lecture followed by discussion, or some other pattern. In some situations, this means that the person in charge of setting up the meeting needs to have clearly in mind what procedure is to be followed. If he announces the expected contract to the group, they are then free to accept, reject, or modify it, negotiating a compromise. It is when the contract is never clarified on either side that difficulty arises.

A group may have several purposes. It may meet for intellectual stimulation as well as personal sharing of feelings. If both purposes are clarified and agreed upon, those who prefer intellectual discussion won't be fighting every time someone shares at a personal level, or the reverse.

Clarifying the purpose does not guarantee harmony or agreement, of course. It is entirely possible for group members to agree upon a purpose for their meetings and then fight to undermine it. I shall never forget a group in which my wife and I once joined several other couples to establish a "depth sharing group." We invited one couple who agreed that they wanted to be a part of such a group. In spite of their apparent agreement, however, this man and his wife fought hard for a more superficial relationship in which members of the group could "just enjoy getting acquainted and being friends." They came with a different contract from the one to which they had given verbal assent. At some unconscious level they had never accepted the stated contract.

As a result of this discrepancy in one couple's "contract-acceptance" level, the group had a built-in conflict which immobilized it for months. When there is a contradiction between the stated purpose and the unconscious operating purpose of an individual, it will probably become visible in his behavior in the group. By seeing that behavior, the other members may be able to help the person realize his problem with the group. An occasional evaluation of behavior in the group can be a valuable experience for everyone.

It is also possible for an entire group to agree upon a stated purpose, but operate on the basis of another goal or purpose which may not be consciously present in the mind of any member, yet may influence all their decisions. An example might be a church couples' club which meets for ostensibly religious purposes, while the need to meet other young couples socially in an inexpensive way may be the real but unstated motivation.

2. The *size* and *composition* of the group should be carefully

considered. Size is an important factor that is often forgotten in the planning of group programs. In the personal groups designed to provide a close, supporting fellowship, size is especially important. For such groups the ideal size is eight to twelve members. A group of six or seven may be strong enough, and a group of fifteen or sixteen may be able to function smoothly, but with each person less than eight or more than twelve the chances for success are probably diminished. A thirteenth person joins the group. Not only is thirteen an unlucky number, but there are now twelve additional relationships to be worked out as number thirteen establishes a relationship with number one, number two, and so on. When a group reaches sixteen or seventeen members, it becomes increasingly difficult for persons to know each other in any depth.

The logical size of a group depends upon several factors. The purpose for which it is organized may dictate how many persons are needed. If the group's purpose is to canvass the neighborhood in search of new church members, then the task may dictate that seventy-five or a hundred persons be involved. If, on the other hand, the object is personal growth for the group members, fifteen should be the maximum size. If the group is to serve as a closely knit education committee, seven or eight may be called for. The most common error I have observed in the formation of personal groups is the tendency to organize them too large for effective sharing and interpersonal relationships. This may be an unconscious effort on someone's part to avoid the intimacy of smaller groups.

Another factor in determining the size of the group should be the skills and resources needed to get the job done. Five or six persons may not have enough dynamic drive and group energy to build low-income housing in the inner city, but may be adequate to a lesser task.

The composition of the group is also important. Some thought should be given to the type of persons who would best suit the purpose of the group. If it is to conduct a senior high canoe trip down the Colorado River, it is probably unwise to invite those over sixty-five years of age to join. Important factors in group composition are age, sex, and educational level. Some people tend to feel that young people should be together, older folks together, and so on. Having experienced both types of group, I am convinced that in most circumstances it is an advantage to include in the same group whenever possible a range of persons old and young, male and female, rich and poor.

Those of us who are older need the stimulation and freshness of the younger generation. Those of us who are young can profit by really listening to the seasoned wisdom of a more experienced person. We men need to understand the feminine point of view, and you women need us as well. Many educated people have the feeling that only college graduates really know what is going on in the world or have worthwhile insights. This is a form of prejudice and is patently untrue, of course. I shall never forget a friend I acquired in a small group whom I shall call Sam. He had grown up in an orphanage, had a modest education, and worked as a laborer in a factory. However, he had a keen mind and read voraciously. He needed little sleep and had a habit of reading into the wee hours of the morning, and listened to many of the serious discussion programs broadcast late at night. He educated himself constantly. Sam knew far more than I about many subjects, and I found him a most stimulating person to know, in spite of his lack of formal education. He and I became good friends, a fact which transcended our racial difference and the discrepancy in our education. I could cite many similar instances from my own experience. For this reason, I feel it is extremely valuable to form groups with a variety of persons rather than try to avoid variety and bring together people who are very similar.

3. The *time factor* is an important element of the group contract. Many groups operate on an announced starting time which no one expects to observe. I recall hurrying my supper one night, jumping into my car, and driving to a 7:30 committee meeting at church. Upon my arrival I discovered that I was the only one present. The other members of the committee straggled in from 7:45 to 8:15. The chairman explained: "We set seven-thirty as the official starting time so we can be sure to get under way by eight o'clock. If we set eight o'clock, we wouldn't get started until eight-thirty." There may be a kind of logic involved here, but logical or not, it wasted half an hour of my time. Members of an ongoing group may profit by discussing a realistic starting time

and agreeing to stick by it so far as possible. When members value their time together and have committed themselves to a specific starting time, they can usually be present and ready to begin by the stated hour.

It is also important to establish a definite stopping time and to honor it. Members will have more respect for the group and for each other if time commitments are honored. A useful pattern some groups adopt is to close the meeting officially at the agreed time. Those who need to leave to keep other commitments may then do so. Those who can linger for a while to chat are free to stay longer, but no essential group decisions should be made after members have left.

How often should the group meet? In addition to establishing starting and stopping times, it is essential to reach an agreement concerning frequency of meetings. Monthly meetings may be sufficient to carry on the business of most boards and committees. However, if the purpose of the group is personal sharing in which individuals are important to each other, this will probably not be adequate. "But people are so busy today," is the usual cry. "They just can't find time to give up more than one night a month." This is simply a myth perpetuated by those who do not want to get close to others. Over and over again, I have seen busy people find the time for anything they really value. Many of the busiest people in our society spend one night a week playing bridge, going to an AA meeting, or attending a personal group that meets their needs as individuals. We make time for the things we really believe in, or that meet our needs at a deep level. One possibility is for a group to agree to meet once a week or twice a month for a few months as an experiment and then reevaluate. When people know that "their group" meets on Thursday nights, they avoid conflicts in advance so they can honor their commitment.

4. It is important for a group to establish the *level of interaction* for its meetings. When this dimension is unclarified, it often leads to misunderstanding and frustration. Let me illustrate by describing three groups.

Group A meets monthly to make decisions concerning the maintenance of the church's property. This group hears a financial report, orders repairs made, plans future renovation, and pays the church's bills. The level of interaction for its meetings is the group task. It is considered inappropriate for Bob to discuss his concern for his sick mother, because the group has a contract to focus on business matters only.

Group B meets monthly as a discussion group. At each meeting one member introduces a topic or reviews a book agreed upon by the group. The group members respond by sharing their ideas about the subject. While the group's purpose is to increase knowledge, their focus is *intellectual content* or ideas. The group considers it inappropriate for George to talk about the need for a new roof on the church, since that is not the contract.

Group C has personal growth as its purpose. Here, Gene discusses his difficulty in getting along with his boss, and the group tries to help him understand the dimensions of his problem. Or Barbara shares her concern about her teen-age daughter, who has been running around with a "gang" of whom she disapproves. The focus for this group is *personal concerns* and *feelings,* and it is considered inappropriate if Mary tries to keep attention focused on a discussion of the Trinity.

I remember well a discussion group in which this level of interaction had never been clarified. One member was constantly frustrated because he had been in a group which shared personal concerns and had found it very meaningful. He had joined the discussion group with the expectation that, as they became acquainted, members would move toward the sharing of feelings. Others in the group had a different contract in mind and were determined to keep the interaction on the level of intellectual content. The group had real difficulty because of this conflict in expectation.

It is entirely possible for a group to combine several levels of interaction in their contract. Some boards of trustees set aside time at every meeting for personal sharing or sharing of ideas about the meanings of their faith. They combine business matters and another focus of discussion in the same meeting. Some groups combine intellectual discussion of their faith with personal sharing on how they have difficulty in living that faith. The important thing is for the group to have a clear agreement on their contract so that expectations are not constantly frustrated.

5. It is essential for every group to have leadership. This is not the same as saying that it is essential for every group to have *a leader*. A group may have excellent leadership without any one person being identified as *the leader*. There are three basic styles of leadership a small group may adopt.

a. It may be organized around an *expert* who serves as leader for the group. The leadership style appropriate for a small group should be clearly related to its purpose. If depth study of the Bible is the purpose, then it may be appropriate for the group to organize around a minister or biblical scholar. If the study of yoga is the object, it may be essential for the group to depend upon a yoga teacher.

b. A second style of leadership common in small groups is the pattern in which the group selects a *chairman*. He (or she) may not be any more expert than the other members, but is chosen to carry out some necessary leadership functions on behalf of the group. He may be outstanding in some respects, but this is not essential to his serving as chairman.

c. A third style used for small groups is *shared leadership*. In this pattern, no one person is designated as more important than the others. The necessary leadership functions are shared by all the members at different times, or there is a rotating temporary chairmanship. In one group to which I belonged, the host couple for the meeting also served as moderators for the meeting when it met in their home. This meant that the wife or husband would open the meeting and provide some minimal leadership to see that the group moved from discussion to business matters (such as where they would meet next time) and closed on time. In another group, when a particular topic or book had been agreed upon, some member who was interested in that book or issue would agree to do some preparation and lead the discussion that night. The discussion leader would change for the next meeting.

A more complete discussion of group leadership will be reserved for Chapter V, but a few important points should be mentioned here. First, it is important that the group have clear agreement as to what its leadership style will be and why. Many ministers, unaware of leadership dynamics, come into every group expecting to be regarded as the *expert leader*.

I remember well my first experience as a pastor in organizing a Bible-study group. My initial impulse was to honor the group by presenting some learned lectures on the passages I had chosen for them to study. I soon discovered that this approach created no magic and interest was not terribly high. I had come into the group assuming that I should function as the expert leader because of my status as pastor and my years of biblical studies. I learned, however, that when members of the group shared the leadership of the sessions and did their own digging for information, interest was higher. When a group has the privilege of deciding upon the appropriate leadership pattern to meet its own goals, involvement will almost certainly be higher. If members agree that an expert leader is needed to accomplish their ends, they will be more likely to accept the leadership and cooperate with it than when it is imposed upon them. Or if people are initially offered a contract which stipulates that Bible study is the purpose and that an expert leader will lecture, they can decide to come or not on that basis. Again, when leadership approaches are not clarified and people come with varying expectations, frustration is almost certain.

6. The sixth element of the group contract is that of *group disciplines*. Most successful groups are those in which the group members have agreed upon some common disciplines they will all observe. They may agree on fairly elaborate disciplines, like the following from a group I once joined. We agreed

   a. to attend all meetings of the group if at all possible,

   b. to read the material agreed upon by the group prior to the discussion,

   c. to pray regularly for each other member of the group,

   d. to begin and close each meeting with five minutes of silence, and

   e. to have coffee available but to serve no food at meetings.

When a group asks nothing of its members, then little may be expected in return. When the members have agreed on their own disciplines, they have something invested in the group and are likely to respect those commitments. On the other hand, if the disciplines are imposed by someone without a group decision involved, resistance may be expected.

In addition to the six basic contract elements outlined, groups tend to make some informal decisions that are influential. Some of these, while never openly mentioned, become operating laws or *norms* of the group's life. For example, a norm of confidentiality may emerge. An understanding may arise in the course of the group's meetings that members will not repeat personal information that is shared in the group. Many groups begin with an unspoken recognition of this norm. In others, it may become a norm simply by one member mentioning it: "I know that none of you will mention this outside the group, or I wouldn't bring it up."

Another norm which often emerges without a vote being taken is that of frankness. If people trust each other, they may feel free to use more everyday language and speak their honest convictions more easily than they would in a formal gathering.

Groups also tend to establish norms concerning the expression of anger and of sympathetic warmth. Some persons and some groups have great difficulty in expressing honest anger. Others are free in their openness with hostility, but have great difficulty in expressing warm feelings. Some groups level off at a "peace at any price" norm and punish any member who tends to express angry feelings. In others, members feel free to clobber each other verbally but frown on the person who expresses tenderness. The mature group—like the mature person—is probably one in which both anger and warmth can be shared with each other.

In establishing such norms, groups tend to take on a distinctive style of their own, or a *group personality*. Sensitive individuals who cannot tolerate conflict may withdraw from a group without knowing consciously why, if some members have the freedom to express and work through conflict. Others may sense the warmth in a group and recoil from it because they are threatened by too much intimacy. The establishment of these norms or elements of group personality is not usually part of the formal contract agreed upon by members, but may be thought of as the *informal contract* which emerges gradually but has deep influence on the group's life.

Those who are concerned with leading small groups or who

are members of them may find it useful to prepare copies of a group contract checklist. This may be especially helpful in the early stages of group life to clarify the important decisions that need to be made. The following form may be used or adapted if it seems useful.

GROUP CONTRACT CHECKLIST

1. Purpose of the group:

2. Meetings: when?_____ how often?_____

    begin _____ a.m. p.m.   close _____ a.m. p.m.

3. Proposed size of group: minimum _____maximum_____

    Composition of group: open to_____

    _____

4. Level of group interaction:

    _____ business matters

    _____ discussion of ideas

    _____ personal sharing

    _____ other: _____

5. Leadership pattern: leadership of the group will

        reside in _____

6. Group disciplines agreed upon:

    _____

    _____

    _____

    _____

7. Other decisions agreed upon:

    _____

    _____

_____

CHAPTER III

EVERY GROUP HAS DYNAMICS

The scene is the weekly staff meeting of a large downtown church. The senior pastor, Robert Wilson, is discussing a program proposed by two of his staff members—Chris Thompson, his associate, and Mary Jane Lewis, his director of religious education.

CHRIS: So we feel that there would be some real advantages in spending a series of weekend retreats with the lay leaders of our congregation. We could set up the first one for October, then follow up with another in January, and . . .

ROBERT: Well, Chris, I'm not exactly sure I see the value of exposing all these people to a program in group dynamics. I know it might be interesting to you, but . . .

MARY JANE: Bob! We're not proposing a program in "group dynamics." We're proposing a program of leadership education! We would use some of the insights from group dynamics, but . . .

ROBERT: Mary Jane, if you are going to use insights from group dynamics, I don't see how you can avoid calling it a group-dynamics program. And if you label these meetings "leadership education" as an excuse to expose these people to group dynamics, I think you're asking for trouble.

CHRIS: I think we may be operating on different definitions of group dynamics, Bob.

ROBERT: How would you define it then?

CHRIS: Do you think we have group dynamics right here in this meeting?

ROBERT: No, I would say this is a staff meeting very much like our other staff meetings. And we have some important business we must finish up this morning. Mary Jane, how are you coming on securing teachers for the church school for fall?

Many people still talk about group dynamics as something interesting which they would rather do without, like poison ivy or the mumps. They say things like "Group dynamics is a way of manipulating a group into doing what you want." Or they will say, "I'm not interested in group dynamics; it's too gimmicky." Like Pastor Wilson, they are identifying group dynamics with a particular set of techniques or gimmicks they have been exposed to somewhere.

Group dynamics is not something you can have or not have. Group dynamics are. Every group has dynamics! There were dynamics present in the church staff meeting just described. For example, the pastor may have felt a challenge to his authority by the two staff members who proposed to do something new. An element of competitiveness was present, and some irritation on the part of the younger staff. In every group dynamic relationships exist—constantly changing—between all the members of the group.

No individual can say, "I'm not interested in personal psychology; I don't think I'll have any." To say we don't want a personal psychology is to say we don't want to exist. The same with groups —you can't have a group without dynamics being present. Dynamics are to a group as the skeleton and muscles and tissues are to the body. The dynamics are the forces that operate to hold the group together and determine the quality of its life. Those dynamics may be positive, negative, or neutral. When they are positive and people in a group seem to be getting along happily and productively, there is little need to be concerned about the dynamics of the situation. However, when the interaction between group members is negative and unproductive, or even neutral and lukewarm, we need to know what processes are blocking communication.

Just as we all have personality dynamics, whether we choose to be aware of them or not, so every group has dynamics. We can ignore these processes, or we can choose to be aware of them and how they are influencing us.

There is an important rule of thumb, tested by research: *When informed attention is paid to group processes, the chances increase that a group will be able to reach maturity and fulfill its potentialities.*

On the other hand, when a group ignores the dynamic processes that influence its life, the chances increase that those dynamics may block the group at some crucial point. It is for this reason that we urge leaders and members of small groups to be aware of these common processes so that they may be utilized for constructive rather than destructive ends. To illustrate: Can you imagine how you would feel if you had been Chris or Mary Jane in the staff meeting reported above? Can you feel into their feelings when they had carefully planned a new design only to have the pastor turn to other business without really hearing them out? I know how I'd feel. I'd be frustrated and angry. I would feel that my expertise was not being honored, and I'd feel like fighting or walking out. Knowing my humanity, I suspect I might find myself resisting the other business matters on the agenda or fighting Mr. Wilson's program at some other point.

A BASIC DISTINCTION

A useful basic concept has come to us from the study of small groups. Psychologists expert in this area speak of a group as having two levels of interaction, the *content* level and the *process* level. In the church staff meeting with Pastor Wilson, the *content* was church business and—more specifically—the discussion of a new program in leadership education. On the *process* level, as we have already seen, a number of things were happening. A *leadership struggle* between staff members may have been one reason for Mr. Wilson's resistance to the proposal. *Frustration* and *anger* were building on the process level, and Wilson's ploy in turning to other business may be seen as a form of *flight* from the conflict with his staff, as well as a convenient way to assert himself. Many persons in a group situation focus their attention only on the content and miss the process interaction. This is like going to a smørgasbord table with one's eyes closed. You are bound to miss a lot of goodies. Both content and process are important.

The process level is that of interaction between persons and may involve feelings, actions, and relationships. A great many things go on at the process level in a group. It is not uncommon to have the experience I once had, when I walked into a committee meeting to which I had been invited and sat listening for a while. I was increasingly puzzled as I heard the members constantly change the subject, ignore each other's comments, and pay no attention to the chairman. At such times it is apparent that something is going on at the process level that may have little or nothing to do with the content of the discussion. *When content and process contradict each other or work against each other, it may be essential for a group to examine its behavior.*

I once attended a political rally where, on the content level, the speakers talked as if their candidate were a cinch to win. They assured the assembled crowd of precinct workers that victory was in the bag. However, the prevailing mood among those present was a sober one. Their emotions did not reflect the optimistic, triumphant note of the speakers. They didn't disagree, but neither did they exult. They knew their candidate had little chance against overwhelming odds. There was a clear contradiction between the verbal content and the level of group process. It is apparently a political necessity never to admit defeat or possible defeat.

A perfect example of contradiction between verbal and process levels is the man who insists in a loud voice, with his teeth clenched and his face nearly purple: "I am not angry!" He communicates one thing by his words and another by his appearance and tone, and he should be helped to understand the contradiction in his overall communication.

SOME COMMON DYNAMICS

When we focus on the process level in a small group, we find some common dynamics or patterns of interaction which the average person can learn to recognize. The best way to become sensitized to the dynamics of a small group is to go through an experience in a human relations laboratory or a special course in group relations. The actual experience of being in a group that pauses to consider the immediate dynamics in its midst is the recommended method for learning this material. This book cannot substitute for a laboratory experience. However, it may be helpful to those who have been through group training, or may serve as an introduction to those who have had no opportunity to attend such a laboratory.

1. *Group climate.* Perhaps the simplest example of group process is that of climate.

I once walked into a committee meeting and took a chair. One or two people nodded in my direction, but basically I was ignored. I was a new member of the committee, but the chairman made no effort to introduce me or make me feel welcome. The group conducted its business in a formal, rigid, uninspired fashion. I came away feeling as if I didn't care if I ever attended another meeting of that committee. The *climate* of the meeting was cold and unfriendly, perhaps hostile.

Nearly anyone, after sitting through a group meeting, can tell you in one word what emotional tone prevailed in that group. Some groups communicate an angry atmosphere, and one can feel the hostility or rejection of the group very quickly. Other groups are warm and friendly, or cold and formal, or joyful, or neutral. These are not absolute categories, but merely ways of describing the emotional tone that pervades a group, which may be perceived in the same way by several persons. A group leader may suggest that members be alert for sudden changes in the group climate. If a group that is usually warm and friendly suddenly becomes cold and rejecting, it may be helpful to ask why. It is possible to develop a sensitivity to group climate which may be very useful, since climate may help or hinder the group in reaching its goals.

2. *Patterns of participation.* One of the most significant facts about any group is who does the talking and who does not. If Sam tends to respond to each person who speaks, the pattern would look something like this:

MARY:
SAM:
BARBARA SUE:
SAM:
LARRY:
SAM:

The person who assumes that he has the right to answer everyone or feels the need to do so soon irritates the rest of the members unless he has been granted that special role by the group itself. This is the "little tin god" approach.

Another common pattern of participation is the tendency for a small subgroup to dominate the discussion, shutting out the other members. The silent person who does not speak at all may represent just as much of a threat to the group as the person who dominates the discussion. Until a group understands why a person is silent it may have difficulty in accepting the silent person as a participating member.

Another interesting variation on participation patterns is the person who remains silent for several meetings, then clobbers the group for its inept and inadequate performance. Having contributed nothing, he is now ready to enter the group by criticizing it. This is the "porcupine" approach, in which the person hides under the woodpile, then enters as a bristling character who drives others away. Another type of entry is the one in which the person does not get really involved until there is a fight, then jumps in to defend someone he sees as weak and in need of help. This is the "knight on a white horse" or "red cross nurse" type.

The observant person can detect these patterns of participation by keeping a part of the attention focused on them while participating normally in the group. However, some practice in observing a group will help one to become aware of these dimensions so they can be useful tools in his later group participation. One very simple tool which the average person may find useful in observing patterns of participation is known as the flow chart.

This is made by drawing a line from the person who speaks toward the person to whom he directs his comment. If he makes a comment directed to the whole group, the line may simply end

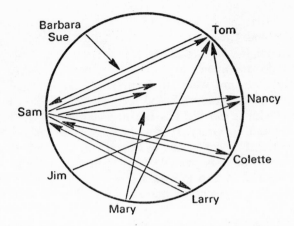

in the middle of the circle. The flow chart should be used for a short period of time, to describe the interaction from 8:15 to 8:30, or 8:30 to 9:00. I have been in groups in which one member presented a flow chart he had been keeping as the group talked, which startled the group into changing its behavior. It was a simple, direct way of revealing that a single member had been dominating the discussion to everyone else's irritation—a fact they were all aware of but did not know how to get at.

3. *Flight and engagement.* One of the most obvious phenomena to observe at the level of group process is that of a group taking flight. I remember some seminary students engaged in serious discussion about their work as student assistants in various churches. Chris introduced an issue that concerned him: the fact that many youth in his church seemed to be involved in premarital sexual intercourse. Henry and Tony made comments indicating that they, too, were faced with this issue and needed some help in thinking about it. This discussion was barely under way when Betty made a remark something like this: "I realize this is an important problem, but I have difficulty discussing it." Immediately Tony said, "I had another problem come up this week, and I'd like to throw it into the hopper." The group instantly latched onto the new topic, and not one member mentioned sex again that day. One interpretation of this event is that the group *took flight* from a touchy

subject like a jet fighter plane taking off from the deck of a sink-
ing aircraft carrier, never to return.

There are many reasons why groups take flight. They may be
avoiding an unpleasant task, they may be setting a limit beyond
which they do not intend to go, or they may simply be resting
after a period of hard work. In fact, groups tend to have a natural alternation between work and rest, or flight from a task and
engagement with it. So flight is not necessarily bad or wrong; it
can be good and necessary. It is when it seems to be an unnecessary avoidance of a "hot" issue, or of conflict, that a question may
be raised about it. It is possible for a group member to say, "I
wonder if we didn't drop that subject too quickly; it may be uncomfortable, but it seems to me we need to take another look
at it."

4. *Leadership competition.* In many groups, there is a designated leader, a clearly established authority in charge. He may be
a teacher or foreman or chairman. If the leader remains clearly
in charge, and this arrangement is accepted by those in the group,
leadership competition may not be a major factor. On the other
hand, if the leader offers a measure of freedom to the group to
participate in sharing the leadership, or if his position as leader is
not very clearly established, one of the most obvious group dynamics is that of leadership competition. By this term I mean simply that various members of the group use ideas and arguments
to defeat the others and establish themselves as the leader. Often
this boils down to a few of the more forceful members, while the
others bow out of the discussion and await the outcome.

The competition may consist of opponents trying to show that
they have more information on the issue at hand than anyone else.
Or it may be a case of one person displaying more aggressiveness
than anyone else in the group. If one member is willing and able
to clobber everyone who disagrees with him, he may become the
dominant member while the others give up in fear and frustration.

A simple way to spot a full-blown leadership battle is to look
for a disproportion in the investment of feelings. I remember a
group in which the members carried on a violent discussion on
Sunday-school teaching. They expressed more anger and took
more extreme positions than their convictions really warranted.

The subject was not important enough to justify so much feeling, and this discrepancy revealed the intensity of the leadership battle in the group. Competition can be good, however, depending upon the situation. It may be good for a group to work through competitiveness so as to reach a more creative level. If it is preventing the group from working at an important task, then it may be negative in character. Calling attention to the presence of competition without judging it as good or bad is sometimes helpful. It can help the group to look more realistically at its own behavior and help some individuals to give up their attempts to dominate and accept the leadership potential in others.

5. *Hidden agenda.* I remember meeting a class the evening following the assassination of President Kennedy. It was obvious from the beginning that the students in that group were not interested in their classwork. An atmosphere of gloom prevailed in the group, and an unwillingness to tackle the subject matter. We had been together only a few minutes when it occurred to me that perhaps the President's death was concerning us all, and we might as well acknowledge the fact and discuss it. I posed this possibility to the group to test my own feelings. They immediately agreed that Kennedy's death was indeed the overriding concern of the group, so we spent the hour sharing our feelings about how the assassination had affected us, how we felt about death, and related matters.

In this instance, the latent feelings of the group about the President's death could be considered a form of *hidden agenda.* Group members came with a concern which was not the explicit agenda of the group, yet which influenced their ability to work as a group. Individuals may come with hidden agenda not shared by others, which can nevertheless influence the task just as directly. I have gone to committee meetings with the hope that the meeting might be over in time for me to get home for my favorite TV show. As a result, my behavior in the group was affected. I wanted decisions made quickly, perhaps at the expense of careful discussion of all the relevant issues. I was more ready to agree with someone just to get it over, and I may have communicated my anxiety to others in the group.

It is not always possible or wise to expose the hidden agendas that are influencing members of a group. But there are times when a group is obviously not doing its job well, and it may help clear the air for someone to ask, "I have the feeling there is something I don't understand that is bothering us tonight, and I wonder if anyone else feels the same way?" Or someone may ask, "We seem to be fighting about everything tonight; is there something we haven't gotten out into the open?" The hidden agendas may take many forms, from individual upset over a crisis in the home to a sense of group bereavement over the loss of a member who has dropped out. It is sometimes helpful to pause in the pursuit of the group task long enough to clarify some of these buried feelings which are blocking the flow of communication. As a friend of mine used to say, "There must be a dead horse in the stream somewhere!" There are also times when the issue is not appropriate for group discussion, and group members will simply have to endure an unsatisfying session together.

6. *The Plop.* I can well recall an occasion on which I offered a group what I thought was an excellent idea, only to have it completely ignored. The excellent idea just fell—PLOP!—right in the middle of the table and sat there. This is a common experience. When one offers two or three ideas in a row only to have them all plop, he begins to question his own sanity. We tend to identify with our ideas, and when they are rejected we tend to feel we have been rejected as persons. There are times when understanding group process can help us understand our plops.

Sometimes we offer suggestions which are ill-timed, for which the group is not ready. It is possible for our ideas to plop under those circumstances. If the group is embroiled in a fierce competition for leadership, and the fight has narrowed to two or three stalwarts, members may be unable to hear suggestions from others in the group because they are not part of the power structure. Or if one person has had more than his share of ideas accepted, they may turn a deaf ear to any more. Groups tend to punish the person who "hogs" more than his share of the discussion. It is also possible that an idea may be excellent, but if accepted would entail a great deal of work or investment of time and energy by the group. They may "fail to hear it" for that reason.

There is another common reason for plops. People often present a suggestion somewhat like this: "I'd like to see our group fly to

Fairbanks for an Eskimo supper." They express an opinion, but fail to ask the enabling question: "Does this appeal to anyone else?" Or "How many like the idea?" When the enabling question is omitted, group members are often unsure what kind of response is expected and remain silent. Result: a big plop. When we find ourselves the victims of several plops in a row, it is sometimes useful simply to ask the group, "Hey, what gives? My last three brilliant suggestions have fallen flat as a pancake. How come?"

7. *Trust level.* Occasionally I work with a group which can plunge immediately into very personal sharing in its first session. The group members act as if they had known each other for years. Other groups have difficulty sharing anything after ten days together. Group members tend to establish a level of trust early in the group's life which determines how much they can share with each other and how deeply they will relate. There are many factors in the calculation of this trust component, but its existence or nonexistence is crucial. People tend to size each other up and evaluate how much they feel they can trust the other person. They probably evaluate, consciously or unconsciously, the person's ability to understand and accept feelings, his rigidity or openness, and his ability to keep confidences. Sometimes the trust level will change radically when an untrustworthy member leaves or a new person joins the group. A crisis which the members share may also deepen the trust level. Like group atmosphere, the trust level is a dimension of group process which the untrained person can be quite aware of simply by listening to his feelings. He either feels the group is trustworthy or he doesn't, though he may not be able to say why.

We know some ways to help groups deepen their level of trust, and these are methods which can be used fruitfully by church groups. One interesting method is called "the process of sharing" and has been tested by careful research.[1] First, each group member is told that he will have a specific amount of time (usually five or six minutes each) in which he is to share one or two incidents from his childhood, one or two from his teen years, and one or two from his adulthood. These should be incidents which he feels have helped to make him the person he (or she) now is.

---

[1] See Herbert A. Otto, "Depth Unfoldment Experience," *Adult Education* (Winter, 1967), pp. 78 ff.

A few minutes are allowed for each person to think about what he might share and jot down a few notes. At the conclusion of the five minutes (and the time limits should be scrupulously observed), each person is asked to share what he considers the happiest moment of his life. It is simply amazing how much closer people feel to each other and how much more deeply they can identify with each other after having gone through this process. It is a method often used with great profit among ministers and laymen in our conferences at the Institute for Advanced Pastoral Studies. It has the limitation of being an entirely verbal exercise, and we now know that when we move past the strictly verbal to include physical contact, trust can deepen even more.

An interesting illustration of the use of physical contact is the trust-circle exercise commonly used now in human relations training. The group stands in a circle with one member in the middle. Keeping his knees stiff and his feet on the floor, the member in the middle falls back so that someone in the group must catch him and pass him to another in the circle. As he is passed around the circle, trusting that the group will not drop him, he feels physically the support he may have suspected the group could not provide. This exercise illustrates the fact that there is a close relation between the physical and the emotional, a relation we have really only begun to discover. Other learnings can emerge from this experience as well. Some people do not want others to get close, and tend to shove them away when they fall in their direction. This helps to raise for them the problem of how they deal with intimacy. By calling attention to how it felt when you were shoved away, you may also help a person to allow more closeness next time. Often he wants people closer to him but is afraid to allow it or doesn't know how. The element of contact in groups will be discussed further in Chapter VIII.

THE IMPORTANCE OF EVALUATION

In his excellent book, *Church Meetings That Matter*,[2] Philip Anderson devotes one full chapter to evaluation, the process by which members of a group review how helpful or fruitful a meet-

[2] Philadelphia–Boston: United Church Press, 1965. Paperback.

ing has been. When people take time to share honestly how they
feel about a meeting, they can discover unrealized values as well
as ways to improve their performance. The keynote is honesty and
frankness. Many people are deathly afraid of being honest with
others. They fear that if they are really honest they may hurt
someone, or the group may reject them. They fail to realize that
honesty is the avenue to deep fellowship and acceptance as well.

I often find myself arguing for honesty in groups in spite of the
possibility that someone's feelings may be hurt. I recall vividly
occasions when some member of a group has told me honestly
how I had been offending him by something I said or did. Those
were painful moments, and they did hurt me. But they were growing moments, as I became more aware of how I might be offending another human being and how I might want to change. A
minister friend recently told me of the old New Englander who
marched up to him one Sunday after the service.

"You use old sermons; I can tell. And another thing. You're
too biblical. We don't know about that stuff. Either teach us about
the Bible or leave it out of your sermons." This bluntness may
horrify some people, but my friend admitted that he needed and
appreciated this man's honesty.

When we are honest with another person, we also risk the possibility that he will reject us and reject the group. However, if you
offer the feedback in such a way that concern is expressed, even
through anger, the person will usually work it through with you.
The person sharing the feedback also risks the possibility that he
is seeing you through prejudiced eyes and that the group may not
support him. In this case, the primary learning may be his own.

Many Christians have the unfortunate idea that to hurt someone
is always un-Christian or unloving. On the contrary, it may be
most loving and Christlike to be honest with a friend by sharing
with him something he needs desperately to know about himself.
I once had a seminary student who communicated an authoritarian arrogance which was very provocative and guaranteed to of-
fend church members and build hostility in his congregation. It
was my responsibility, I felt, to share honestly with him how he
came through to me. When I told him what I saw, he was out-
raged and remained angry with me for months. Finally, the day

came when he was able to admit to himself that he indeed had problems, and he later came in to apologize and thank me for my evaluation. I had to accept his anger and alienation, but in this case the result was worth the risk and the wait. It is sometimes necessary to hurt someone to maintain our own integrity and help them to grow. Bearing the hurt with them is part of what life is all about.

Honesty in evaluating our group meetings is equally important. If we do not care enough about the group to be honest, that in itself is a form of evaluation. Groups often set aside time to review how group members feel about the meeting and to consider how to improve. Philip Anderson's book, *Church Meetings That Matter,* includes a good evaluation form which can be used fruitfully by many types of groups. He offers it to anyone who cares to duplicate it, and I have used it with groups on many occasions myself. I have included an evaluation form of my own at the end of this chapter. This form may also be used freely or adapted to fit the situation.

There is a very simple evaluation method which can be used almost anywhere with profit. A colleague and I found it useful when we arrived in another city to lead some sessions on communication with a group of clergy. They had been sitting all afternoon hearing one presentation after another with no chance to respond. My friend and I felt the growing hostility in the group, and we feared that they would be unable to hear us when we took over for the evening session. As a result, we decided to begin with a period of evaluation. When they gathered, we asked the group to write down the first word that came to their minds when we asked the question, "How do you feel about the program at this conference so far?" As soon as they had taken a moment to write down their word responses, we copied them on the blackboard as they called them out. There were many positive words reported, such as okay, happy, or helpful, some neutral words, and a good many negative words like angry, tired, or frustrated. One honest man even reported a strong word usually associated with barnyards, to the surprise of his superiors. We then allowed the men time to scatter in pairs for a while and talk about why they felt as they did. This procedure seemed to clear the air to some extent, so that we could begin our presentation with more openness and they could feel that their frustrations had been heard as well.

The use of this word-association method of evaluating a group meeting takes very little time, usually reflects honest feelings, and can reveal some important data about the meeting. It is especially helpful if someone asks the group members to say a few words about why they chose the word anger, or what they meant when they reported frustration. No evaluation forms are necessary with this method, and it can be done quickly and easily.

Another easy method is simply to stop the meeting at a stated time and hold open discussion on how the group members feel about it. This is often useful, and again requires no equipment or tabulation. The drawback is that it may lack discipline, with no clear criteria before the group to remind them of a basis for making judgments. For this reason, something like the evaluation form found at the end of this chapter may be useful in order to establish criteria in the minds of group members. After the form has been used a few times, the group can move to open evaluation, with categories such as responsible participation, shared leadership, authenticity, acceptance of persons, productivity, and so on clearly established as goals.

Time for evaluation and willingness to risk honesty can make the difference between a lifeless group and a vital community of sharing persons. The elements of group process listed in this chapter offer some possible areas for discussion in group evaluation when they become obvious problems to a group.

In the following chapter another dimension of group process— the tendency for groups to mature—will be discussed in detail. Some group behavior is very difficult to understand without the information in this next chapter. It should also be noted that there are many dimensions of group process which are not mentioned here. In order to present a few of the most important, I have had to be selective and omit a great many others.

SMALL GROUP EVALUATION SHEET

This is a sample evaluation sheet for use in a variety of small group meetings. It may be copied or adapted without further permission. Group members should simply be instructed to give their honest and immediate impressions in response to the following questions.

IN THIS
MEETING   (Circle one category for each statement)

1. LEADERSHIP WAS	Dominated by one person	Dominated by a subgroup	Centered in about half the group	Shared by all members of the group
2. COMMUNICATION WAS	Badly blocked	Difficult	Fairly open	Very open and free-flowing
3. PEOPLE WERE	Phony	Hidden	Fairly open	Honest and authentic
4. THE GROUP WAS	Avoiding its task	Loafing	Getting some work done	Working hard at its task
5. I FELT	Misunderstood and rejected	Somewhat misunderstood	Somewhat accepted	Completely accepted and understood by the group

6. The one word I would use to describe the climate of this meeting: _____

7. Suggestions:

CHAPTER **IV**

GROUPS MATURE LIKE PEOPLE

One of the most fascinating aspects of small groups is their tendency to mature. This tendency of small groups to "grow up" is strikingly parallel to the growth pattern of the individual. On the level of group process, this *maturing cycle* helps to explain some group behavior which would otherwise remain a mystery. Furthermore, when this process is taken into account, it greatly increases the chances for unlocking the power and potentiality of the small group. It is of great importance in groups of many kinds, from families to nations,[1] and has deep implications for those who are concerned to develop mature church fellowships.

The following is an excerpt from a group leader's diary:

My group behaved in a strange fashion today. In their last meeting, the group seemed quarrelsome and competitive. Today they took me on. They either ignored my suggestions completely or made light of them. The group seemed unable to take me seriously. About halfway through the session, one member of the group asked if it was really true that the group was free to shape its own life. He asked the rest

[1] For the original research upon which this chapter is based, see Warren G. Bennis and Herbert Shepard, "A Theory of Group Development," *Human Relations*, Vol. IX, No. 4 (1956), pp. 415–37. My own version of this pattern is also spelled out in an article, "The Authority Cycle in Small Group Development," *Adult Leadership* (April, 1965) and in "Small Group Insights for the Servant Ministry," *Pastoral Psychology* (April, 1968).

of the group, not me. They assured him that it was true. He then proposed that the group move outside and meet under the trees where it would be cooler. The group enthusiastically shouted their approval of the idea, and they were already on their way out the door before the shouts died down. They laughed and joked and resisted every attempt to introduce a serious topic. I noted with interest that no one bothered to ask me how I felt about the group moving outside. It seemed to be an unspoken agreement that the leader didn't count today.

In actuality, the group behavior described above makes perfect sense when we understand it in the light of the authority cycle or maturing process. It might otherwise be interpreted as irresponsible behavior. I would interpret such behavior as a sign of group strength and growth, and this chapter will attempt to make sense of that paradox.

When small groups are given a measure of freedom, they tend to move through a series of stages in relation to the authority of the leader. We may say that groups tend to move

    a. from *dependence* upon the stated leader,

    b. through a brief period of *resistance to the freedom* offered them,

    c. then through a period of *"adolescent rebellion,"*

    d. until their rebellion wins a significant victory, when they observe a period of *celebration and independence,*

    e. upon which they act more responsibly in a state of *interdependence* with the original leader-authority,

    f. although a crisis may cause the group to fall back to *dependence* and begin the cycle all over.

Each of these stages of development will be discussed in some detail, and the parallel with individual growth and development pointed out. The movement from one stage to another is often subtle and is most easily observed in a laboratory setting. However, when one is sensitized to this dimension in groups, it provides some valuable handles for understanding ordinary group behavior. After the discussion of these various group stages, we may examine some of the implications for the church.

It will be helpful to explain first the meaning of the term "a measure of freedom." Many groups are so structured that they do not have any freedom and do not move through the stages of growth described above. A lecture class in which the group remains dependent upon the lecturer the entire time would be an example of this type of group. The dependence stage may be perfectly appropriate for such a group. In the typical church service, the congregation remains dependent upon the structure of the Mass or the service and the leadership of the clergyman. We all know ministers who prepare the agenda of their church board meetings and have the decisions cut and dried before the group ever meets. Board members often report that they feel like rubber stamps in such situations. Again the group is not given much freedom and remains dependent upon the minister's leadership.

On the other hand, there are many models of groups in which the members themselves are responsible for making decisions that affect the life of the group. The leader or the structure itself has granted them "a measure of freedom." The T-group in a human relations laboratory is an instance of a group which has such freedom, because the trainer permits the group to develop its own agenda. The youth group which is allowed to plan its own program or the committee which shapes its work as a group are further examples of groups with a measure of freedom. The key lies with the leader, who either permits freedom or keeps the group dependent upon his leadership. A Bible-study group in a church may depend upon a minister to make all basic decisions and provide direction, or it may be an interpersonal study group in which the members have a great deal to say about how the group is run and what is discussed. It will be assumed throughout the rest of this chapter that we are talking about situations in which the leader intends the group to exercise some freedom, so that the maturing process may appear.

CHARACTERISTICS OF GROUP STAGES

a. Dependence. This is the starting point of most human groups. The group is assembled around a common purpose and looks to a designated leader to kick things off. When a new group of conferees arrives at the Institute for Advanced Pastoral Studies, they instinctively wait for the director to make announcements and tell them what to do next. Group members and the group as a whole are dependent upon the leader for guidance, even though the group may include seminary presidents, ministers and priests, professors, and others accustomed to leadership. This dependence is indicated in a number of ways: raising the hand for the recognition of the leader, looking at the leader while speaking, turning to the leader with all questions, asking him for help, or looking in the direction of the leader expecting him to act.

Perhaps the classic example of dependence is the typical classroom situation in which the leader stands before the class in a slightly elevated position with all chairs facing him. He is the maker of decisions that affect the group, the dispenser of rewards and punishments.

In the human individual the parallel to this stage is the infant-parent relationship, in which the small child is clearly dependent upon the leadership and protection of the parent. The parent must provide the child's basic needs or he will perish.

It is rather difficult to imagine a group in diapers, but groups experience an infancy in many ways. It is at the point of the group's infancy that it is appropriate for the leader to act somewhat as a parent. There are many situations where dependence is appropriate or even necessary to accomplish the intended purpose. The danger for parents and for group leaders is the seductive tendency to prolong dependence far longer than necessary. It is often difficult to give up the pleasurable position as the leader upon whom others are dependent. In the name of leadership the authority-hungry person often maintains a group at the dependence level and effectively prevents the growth of its members, just as some parents cannot give up their "babies." They remain "babies" even when they march off to college. An important leadership quality is to know how much freedom to give a group and how soon the group is ready to use it creatively.

Dependence can be a comfortable state for both leader and group. Many groups are perfectly content to let their leader do all their work, make all their decisions, and leave them alone. Such a group may be unprepared, however, if it should suddenly be necessary for them to assume some responsibility. Many congregations have found themselves in precisely that position when a strong authoritarian leader suddenly leaves after years of making all their decisions for them.

b. Resistance to freedom. When a group is first offered freedom, or when freedom is thrust upon a group by the leader, the initial reaction is often one of resistance and hostility. Tradition and experience have led people to believe that a leader should provide direction and the group members accept it. They become anxious when the leader throws them the ball and their expectations are not met. In particular the more dependent members of the group will be opposed to this unwanted freedom. They are people who prefer a comfortable leader-centered situation, and to discover suddenly that they share responsibility for the life of the group is intolerable. They may fear that they will be exposed in some way through participation, and thus prefer to remain in the wings while the leader holds center stage. So we find groups expressing feelings of hostility and resistance toward the leader who has granted them the freedom to shape their own destiny.

It is comparable to rolling the stone away from the entrance of a cave in which some men have been imprisoned without light for years. We expect them to rush out into the sunlight, praising their benefactor and rejoicing in their newfound freedom. Instead they cower in the back of the cave, shielding their eyes from the light and cursing the fool who has blinded them without warning.

Some ministers have discovered that this principle applies to committees and congregations as well. Many of them leave a conference at the Institute for Advanced Pastoral Studies determined to introduce sermon discussion when they get home. Phil is typical. He returned home, and the following Sunday he stopped in the middle of his sermon and said, "Now what questions do you have about this morning's message?" He was met by a stunned silence, and after thirty seconds of awkward waiting, he announced the closing hymn. Several parishioners told him after the service that this had made them angry. Phil never tried sermon discussion again, because he had been unprepared for the initial resistance one may expect under such conditions. In addition, Phil failed to prepare the congregation and involve them in the innovation, nor did he have the courage to wait out their initial resistance so the change could have a fair trial.

Many leaders have been stunned by this initial wave of hostility when they have tried to offer freedom and responsibility to their laymen, and have retreated to a more authoritarian style, hurt and puzzled. They have been told by their seminary professors to free the ministry of the laity, but they have not learned the realities of coping with resistance to change. They are not taught to expect this initial hostility and are not prepared to accept it and use it creatively.

The analogy at the level of individual growth may be the point at which the child is willing to enter the door of the nursery school, but does not want his mother to go away and leave him there alone. He says he wants to grow up and start to "school," but clings to his mother's leg in fear at the same time.

The group leader who can understand the meaning of this initial resistance and accept it without being defensive can help his group move on to the next stage. The mother who will not leave her child at the nursery school because he is crying is in for a long year with a dependent child. Similarly, the group leader who backs off in dismay at the initial refusal of a group to take hold of responsibility may be left with a dependent group.

c. Adolescent rebellion. The rough waters of the initial resistance phase give way to storms of rebellion in the next phase. When a group has finally accepted the fact that it has some freedom to determine its own life, it begins to move away from the leader and make some decisions of its own. It may have insisted that the leader structure the situation. Finding that he will not do it for them, the group gives up its resistance to freedom and begins to move toward independence from this leader-who-won't-lead-as-expected. When a group senses that it is strong enough, the movement toward independence begins. Indeed, some individuals in it may have been moving that way from the very beginning.

There are three characteristics of this rebellious phase. The first is the intensification of leadership struggle within the group. When it has become obvious that the established leader is not going to provide all the decisions and answers, members begin to move into the leadership vacuum and vie with one another for prominence. When this struggle among the giants is at least partially resolved, the group is in a better position to take on the established leader and settle matters with him.

A second characteristic of the rebellious phase is the establishment of some minimal norms and patterns of procedure. When the group finds that it can make some procedural decisions on its own, this reduces anxiety and provides some security and strength.

The third characteristic is the expression of hostility and rejection toward the leader-who-did-not-lead. However, it is hostility for a purpose—the positive life-giving purpose of thrusting away from dependence toward independence. It is saying in effect to the leader, "All right, if you're not going to do the job for us, we'll show you that we can get along without you."

The traits, then, of this rebellious phase, which is often called *counterdependence* by group workers, are both positive and negative. On the negative side it is most readily identified by hostile comments directed toward the leader. These may be very subtle, on a subconscious level, but clearly antagonistic. Group members may be heard to say things like "When I was in a group like this out in Berkeley last year, we had a leader who was really dynamic; he sure knew what he was doing." "I wonder what would happen if we didn't show up next time."

The group's rebellious feelings may also be expressed in unconscious group behavior such as ignoring the leader's comments and otherwise resisting the program he represents.

This counterdependent hostility is occasionally expressed in a dramatic symbolic form. One of the most vivid instances I recall was the time I was symbolically "buried" by a group. We had been experimenting with some exercises in which we picked up members of the group and rocked them. One member of my group asked me, "Wouldn't you like to be picked up?" I said, "Yes, I'd like that." So I lay down flat on the floor, and the group members gathered around and picked me up. As they did so, one of the members said, "Let's take him outside." The group accepted this suggestion with alacrity and carried me out onto the terrace. Someone then said, "Let's throw him over the side." So they swung me as if they were going to fling me over the terrace. Oh, cruel fate! They then laid me down on the cement terrace and gathered around the "corpse." Someone folded my hands together reverently, while another placed a symbolic flower on my chest. Then they walked off laughing. It was all done in "good fun," but I also felt the symbolic rejection of the leader as an expression of group strength, and I recalled that some group psychotherapists speak of the "ritual death of the leader" as a common theme in therapy groups.

The tendency for the leader to fight the group or insist on the validity of his viewpoint, in order to keep the group dependent upon his leadership and guidance, is strong at this stage. *If the leader does not grant the group freedom to express its hostility and rejection of him, its growth may be virtually ended here.*

The positive aspects of the rebellious phase are represented by the fact that the group is beginning to take responsibility for its own life. It may make a minor decision, like agreeing to meet outside under the trees, which represents a rejection of the leader and an affirmation of group strength. As the decision is made, the group becomes independent to some extent.

On the individual level, this rebellious phase is readily observable in the agonies of the teen-ager struggling to free himself from dependence upon his parents.

The situation is one of dual ambivalence. The teen-ager wants his independence, yet fears that he may achieve it before he is ready. At the same time, the parents want to see their child grow up, yet fear to lose him. The teen-ager often engages in extreme criticism of his parents, bugging them about their clothes, their moral standards, their automobile. He is testing to see how much freedom he has and how much he can manage. His rebellion against parental controls is comparable to the rebellion of the group seeking to free itself from dependence upon the leader. The emotional dynamics between the leader and his group may be exact parallels of the dynamics the group members have experienced with their parents. The transfer of authority feelings and authority problems to new authority figures is a common feature of human interaction.

It cannot be stated too emphatically that the teen-ager's rebellion is both natural and healthy *within reasonable limits*. It is the only way he can find life and creative freedom. Similarly, the rebellious behavior of a small group toward its leader may be the healthy expression of its growth toward maturity and away from stifling dependence. For this reason, the group leader must be willing to suffer the pain of his group's hostility in order to help the group to freedom. This pain may be very mild, but it can be traumatic at times. Many group leaders are unwilling or simply unable to bear it, and they retreat at the point of greatest promise for their group.

This is the level at which many committees and their chairmen, or ministers and their boards, become stuck in a continuing and futile power struggle. The leader, unwilling to accept the pain and risk of allowing the group to establish its independence, fights to keep his dominant role. The group, unwilling to remain dependent upon him, jockeys for position on every issue—all clothed in politeness, of course. For that reason it is very important for group leaders of all sorts to learn to recognize the subtle expressions of "adolescent rebellion" and accept the accompanying hostility (which really hurts), in order to free a group for its most creative work.

d. Celebration and independence. In the very act of expressing its rebellious feelings, a group is declaring its independence of the leader. If the leader is able to accept this declaration and grant the group its freedom, it can enter a new phase of its existence. The independence stage is basically a brief celebration and is characterized by an atmosphere of joy, laughter, and giddy behavior. A decision by the group which runs somewhat counter to the position of the established leader may be the symbolic act which ushers in this stage of independence and tips off the celebration. In the excerpt from a group leader's diary cited at the beginning of this chapter, the group was declaring its independence and celebrating its freedom. The group's behavior doesn't make much sense without this framework to put it in perspective.

During this phase, the leader is often ignored completely, as though the group were saying in effect, "See, we don't need you. We can do this ourselves." In the giddiness of this newfound freedom, they often discuss a topic no one is really interested in, and talk about it to the point of exhaustion just to prove they have the freedom to do so. There is also a tendency to resist serious business which might disturb the pleasurable flight from reality in which they are engaged.

On the individual level of personality growth, the classic parallel to this stage is the youth who goes away to college and rejects many of his family's norms in the process. If his family is religious, he becomes agnostic or atheistic. If the family is Republican and conservative, he becomes a liberal or a radical. If the family is church-oriented, he avoids the campus churches and student religious foundations like poison. He gets drunk and stays out all night, not just because he enjoys it (which he may not), but simply to prove that he has the freedom to do so. Serious study may be considered an intrusion by the young student in the heat of this declaration of independence.

Beyond accepting their initial resistance and hostility, then, the leader who would free his group needs to accept that which is most difficult of all: the group's rejection of his leadership. He needs to help them express their angry, rebellious feelings and reach a degree of independence from himself in order to free their creative leadership potential. In a deep sense, this is bearing the cross. This is the suffering servant role—the dying unto self—which initially made the Christian Church possible. Most ministers, like most persons, tend to shrink from this pain. They have not been led to expect it; they have not been trained to bear it—and so they revert to a dependence relationship which is basically sterile.

e. Interdependence. As a group acts out its independence, there is an aura of unreality about its behavior. Not only is it ignoring the leader—it is denying the contribution he could be making to the group and the fact that he is still in some undefined way their head. Once the group has been allowed its freedom, however, an interesting development tends to take place. Having proven that it truly does have freedom, it now tends to begin taking that freedom seriously and responsibly.

The group has now entered the *interdependent* stage, which has greater potentiality for creative and constructive work. A dramatic change of atmosphere may occur. The group ceases to fight the leader and permits him to reenter, with his legitimate contribution. It begins to acknowledge the real contribution he is able to make and to take advantage of his special knowledge and insight rather than seeing him as a threat or an enemy. The group members become interdependent in relation to each other and to the original leader, and shared leadership tends to predominate.

Characteristics of this stage of group life include a more subdued and considerate tone in the discussion. Group members are better able to hear each other and competition seems to fade into the background. Ideas are weighed more carefully than before and honesty is more common. Discussion tends to be on a deeper, more personal level, and morale is generally high. Smooth functioning and a high rate of productivity are often the result. There is a joyous quality about the interpersonal relationships within the group when the members have suffered through to this point together.

The characteristics of the interdependent stage of group life are powerfully parallel to the characteristics of the ideal Christian community or *koinonia* one reads about in theology textbooks but rarely finds incarnated!

On the individual level, this stage is illustrated by the college graduate who now has a wife and a job and comes back home to sit down over a glass of beer and smoke a cigar with the "old man" on a basis of personal equality. Father is still honored as father, but the authority relationship is changed. There are now two authorities in place of one.

If the interdependent stage is truly the most creative and productive stage of group development, it becomes apparent how important it is for group leaders to help the movement of a group to this level. It should also be noted that this is the stage at which it is easiest for a leader to pull out and leave the group to continue as an autonomous unit, while the leader is freed to initiate new groups. For organizations such as the churches, which rely heavily on lay leadership, this insight may be of crucial importance, and particularly so if a clergy shortage is to be anticipated.

CHARACTERISTICS OF THE CYCLE

The above description of the movement from dependence to interdependence suggests that a group moves steadily and smoothly from the first stage to the last. While it is possible for this to happen, there are various other possibilities. For example, a group can complete a cycle from dependence to interdependence and fall back to dependence upon the leader within one meeting. It may then begin the cycle over again—all in one session. Or the group may reach only the rebellious stage, when the panic of an individual or a crisis in the group causes it to fall back to dependence. (Similarly, the mature adult may reach a crisis in life, such as a heart attack, and find himself once more in childlike dependence upon his parents.) The more dependent individuals in the group may occasionally turn to the leader with comments such as, "I'd like to ask our leader what he thinks," or "Why not ask our leader to bail us out of this one?" The leader may also welcome this invitation to give a little speech or encourage dependence upon his leadership for a short time in other ways.

Once a group has worked through its initial resistance to freedom, it will tend to move more rapidly through the cycle after returning briefly to the dependence stage. As the group gathers strength, it may jump from a brief period of dependence back to interdependence, skipping the intermediate stages. On the other hand, some groups get stuck permanently at a particular stage and never complete the cycle. The possible variations on this theme are infinite.

Another fascinating observation from my experience is that groups begin at a much deeper trust level when they have some nonverbal contact experiences early in their life together. When they begin with strictly verbal encounter, it takes much longer to work through the maturing process and reach interdependence. The nonverbal approach seems to short-cut this process, for reasons I do not fully understand. Exercises such as the trust circle, described elsewhere in this book, or other experiences such as those described in Chapter VIII, are helpful in this regard.

It should also be remembered that some individuals within a group move more rapidly or more slowly than the group as a whole. Some may be so dependent that they remain at that level while the group moves on. Others may have so much hostility toward authority figures that they never get past the rebellion stage, continuing to fight the leader and refusing to join the movement to interdependence.

Those whose goal in working with groups is to release leadership potential may well heed the tendency of groups to move through this cycle of growth. At the same time as they work to free people from dependence upon them, they will need to remember that many church people have years and years of personal history as dependent receivers. It will require patience and time to help them grow into interdependent givers who share the ministry and leadership of the church.

In the emerging concept of ministry as servanthood, the minister's role is parallel or analogous to that of the small group leader in many ways. The minister, like the small group leader, needs to help his people work through their interpersonal conflicts in order to reach a depth of honesty and love, or the result is a group which settles for a superficial level of relationships. Tension and conflict are too often avoided in the church at a cost of deep and honest relationships. Or they are avoided until they explode and cause great damage to persons. So the minister's task may be seen as an effort to free his people from dependence and help them to discover their mutual ministry. He must lose his life as the absolute leader, the one who stands at the center of all activity and makes all the decisions. Only in this way can he find a more exciting and demanding concept of ministry as servant, releasing the ministry of others.

CHAPTER V

THE LEADER OF THE
SMALL GROUP

As he drove through the light evening traffic to the church, Keith Thompson was thoughtful. What was to be his role tonight? George Hilton and Don Smith had both spoken to him about the meeting and asked for some help in getting a new group started. He recalled how Don had put it: "Keith, some of us feel the need for a deeper spiritual pilgrimage. We just don't find that on Sunday mornings, and ushering doesn't satisfy this hunger. Teaching Sunday school doesn't seem to do it either. We'd like to start a new group and we need your help. Could you meet with some of us on Friday night?"

Keith remembered his reaction. Another meeting! His heart sank. Yet there was a gleam of hope in this man's yearning. His church members often seemed uninterested in "spiritual" matters, so this sounded promising. Since coming to Redeemer Church as pastor four years before, he had constantly hoped for something new and creative to break loose, but found himself bogged down in the administrative job of keeping a marginal church afloat. There just hadn't been much time for new creative ventures. He glanced at his wife, seated beside him in the car, and smiled. He had told her about the Friday meeting, expecting another familiar reaction, "Oh Keith, not another evening away from the family!" Instead, she asked more questions and then inquired if she could come too. This had both surprised and pleased him. Perhaps this would be one thing they could do as a couple that would bring them closer together. Don, when he called back, had been delighted that Betty would join them. He said that there would be four couples and George Hilton—George's wife just wasn't interested, but George was coming anyway.

And so Keith pondered the meeting ahead as he and Betty cruised along West Tenth Street toward the church. Just how much leadership would he be expected to provide? His inner doubts were not reflected in his outward appearance of omniscience. He didn't really know much about the type of interpersonal spiritual search group they seemed to want. Perhaps they would expect more of him than he could deliver. He might even look foolish, if he had to pretend to know more than he did. He would just have to be honest with them! Even if it meant being knocked off his pedestal as an expert, it was far better just to admit that there were some things he didn't know. It might hurt his pride a bit, but integrity was more important.

Another question crossed his mind. What kind of leadership was called for at a meeting of this type? He really couldn't be the expert, the "answer man," anyway, but would it be appropriate even if he could? Probably not. His role was probably to help the group clarify what they were after and where some of the resources could be found to meet their needs. In fact, he would have to be careful not to get sucked in, trapped into being the "leader." Keith realized that far too often he let himself dominate at meetings. He didn't want to, but it just happened. He had a hard time stopping himself from talking too much. He got started and just couldn't quit. And people seemed to appreciate his taking the lead. But he knew that Don and George had a different kind of group in mind, and he would have to take care not to talk too much. It would be much more productive if they all shared the leadership. After all, some of these people were pretty sharp, with plenty of leadership potential. Why should he be the "big daddy" for a group like that? He would play it cool and see what happened.

Beside him, his wife Betty was hoping the meeting would go well. In particular, she hoped her husband would not dominate the meeting and discourage the others from talking. Too often she had seen him overpower the others at a meeting by knowing more, talking more, and using up all the time. She would see their faces slowly sag, until they left saying the right polite words. But they went home with an air of resignation that meant they had lost interest and probably wouldn't be back. He seemed to gain strength from being at the center of the group, and he would go away from the meetings pleased and happy. She had tried to help him understand that the others were not as happy, but they always denied it if he asked them. After all, you don't talk to a clergyman that way. You smile and keep your mouth shut.

In another car a few blocks away, Don Smith and his wife Eugenia were also approaching the church. Don had high hopes for the meeting. "I think we've really got something going, Gene," he said. "The Prices will be there and the Cottons. Betty Thompson's coming with Keith because she's interested in the group herself. I hadn't expected that. And, of course, George. We may pick up a few more next time."

"If only you can keep the pastor from running the whole show," she said. "That will kill it for sure. He has a lot to offer—but does he have to offer it all the time?"

"I know what you mean, honey, and George and I are determined not to kowtow to him just because he is the pastor. We want him to offer guidance, but we won't let him run things. If we have to be blunt about it, we will. This is too important to let Keith spoil it, however well-meaning he is."

"So who is going to lead this little venture?"

"The way I see it, we don't need any one person to be leader. We're adults and we can make the necessary decisions together. I've agreed to serve as chairman tonight just to get the show on the road, but that's not a permanent job."

The case illustration reported above illustrates some of the important dimensions involved in small-group leadership. One of the most pervasive problems confronting church members is the "holy man" syndrome. The feeling that the clergyman should be turned to as *the leader* for everything is unfair to both minister and people. It puts an impossible burden on him, for no man is expert in every phase of religious life. And it cheats the lay person, depriving him of the opportunity to grow into spiritual maturity. Learning to cope with these unreal expectations of leadership is a very real problem for both. The minister is ambivalent about giving up his comfortable spot on the throne, even while he yearns to see his people grow. Laymen find it easier not to challenge him, even while they earnestly want a more significant role for themselves.

We shall now examine the two major options available for the leadership of small groups, expert leadership and shared leadership. After these two approaches have been delineated, I will outline another important concept, that of leadership flexibility, which helps to keep the two options in perspective.

THE EXPERT LEADER

I sat in the back row and observed as the Reverend Mr. Conklin led his weekly Bible study group.[1] For about thirty minutes, he spoke about the assigned passage, while the group members listened and occasionally consulted the Bibles open in their laps. Some took notes as he talked. Mr. Conklin sat at the front, facing the group members who were in three rows, classroom style. About twelve persons were present that evening. When Mr. Conklin finished his remarks, several ladies asked questions and one of the men commented about the passage and its meaning for him. Each in turn addressed his remarks to Mr. Conklin, who responded before turning to the next speaker.

Mr. Conklin's style in this case was one of *highly focused expert leadership*. Leadership was focused in Conklin, except when a group member offered an insight from his own experience. Even then, Conklin retained the power to approve or veto, as well as the power to grant permission to speak at all. There are many situations where this approach is legitimate and appropriate, especially when one person has expert information which the others desire to share. This leadership style may be considerably varied, as in the case of Paul Wilson, leader of a discussion group organized to discuss religious concerns. Paul also began each session with a brief presentation to open up the subject. In his case, however, he spoke only five minutes, then opened the discussion to the group. Group members were seated in a circle rather than in rows, so they quickly began to speak to one another as well as to Paul. Paul would occasionally intervene, particularly when he felt that the discussion was straying from the subject. At the close of the period, Paul summarized the discussion and made a few closing remarks. He remained in the role of expert leader, but allowed more group participation and was more flexible than Conklin had been.

[1] The descriptions in this section are based on live observations, but names are disguised in each instance.

It may well be that Conklin has stronger personal needs to dominate, while Wilson might have greater need for warmth. There is nothing wrong with having needs, and with recognizing ourselves for what we are. When our leadership needs are met on the other side by equivalent needs on the part of our followers, we may have a creative situation. It is when our needs come first with little or no consideration of the needs of others that we create difficulty. If Mr. Conklin maintains an iron-hand style of leadership in which only his ideas are acceptable, he may satisfy some deep needs of his own, but he may be squelching the aspirations of his group members to grow.

Another variation of the expert leader role is that of *resource* person. I observed a young pastor, Jim Schneider, as he exemplified this approach. Jim met regularly with a group of women in his church for prayer and Bible study. However, one of the ladies, Mrs. Thompson, served as chairman of the group and called the meeting to order. After some preliminaries were disposed of, she asked Jim if he would lead the group in prayer. He led with a brief spoken prayer, then invited group members to add their prayers. Mrs. Thompson then led the discussion of the passage from Scripture, and only twice during the meeting did she turn to Jim as biblical authority to help clear up a point of misunderstanding. He was helpful on one point, but confessed that he did not know the answer on the other. The resource person offers his expertise when it is appropriate, but refrains from dominating the leadership of the group. As he told me, there were many occasions when he could not be present at meetings of this group, but his absence did not hinder their progress.

There is yet a third alternative under the expert leader category, and it is one I use often. When I meet with a marathon group which is under contract to stay together without break for a long period, for example, I initially assume a fairly active role. I provide clear structure for the group, and I do not hesitate to set limits when I feel they are needed. At the same time, I try to free the group members so they can interact with each other, not just with me. I help them move from the more focused leadership I have provided to a genuinely shared leadership, although I stand ready to step in whenever I feel it is necessary. I never cease to be leader of the group, which is my assigned responsibility, but I help others to share that leadership as much as possible. The leadership does not remain highly focused in me, nor am I simply a resource person. This is a very active role, and requires one to bring his full strength and authority to the task. It may be designated as *parental leadership,* for the role is comparable to that of the parent. The mature parent, after all, provides structure and limits for his children, but helps them become independent of him as they are able. At the same time, the leader is a full participant in the group. He shares his concerns, confesses his needs, and admits his humanity as he contributes to the life of the group. He doesn't hold himself aloof as a distant observer, but is a full leader/participant.

I submit that this parental leadership style has value as a basic model for those who work with congregations and with many other types of groups. This style involves movement from highly focused leadership to shared leadership—all within one consistent leadership approach. It is to the concept of shared leadership that we now turn our attention.

THE SHARED LEADERSHIP CONCEPT

In discussing the elements of a group contract, shared leadership was mentioned as one option, and the term has often been used in this book. What does it really mean, and how is it possible? We begin with the fact that the term leadership is being radically redefined in our time. In the old definition, it was a quality which a person either had or didn't have. Leaders were born, not made. It was assumed that if leadership was really a personal quality, some research methods could be found which would point out future leaders and nonleaders. The army in particular has wanted to identify potential leaders. They could then put them into officer training and save money by training only men who can lead. Great sums of money have been spent in research to identify the traits of a leader, but no correlation was ever discovered that permitted the prediction of future leaders. This way of understanding leadership has now been replaced by a new concept: that leadership consists of a series of *functions.* Let me use an example.

Keith and Betty Thompson arrived at the church to find the others there ahead of them. As they sat down, members of the circle spent time greeting each other, asking about each other's children, commenting on Betty's new hairdo, and complimenting George on his new lime-green turtle-neck shirt. At that point, a leadership function was needed. Someone had to *initiate* the introduction of the evening's business. Don, the chairman or designated leader, might have done it. Keith could have done it. In fact, any member of the group could have served this function, but it was George who said: "Why don't we get this show on the road?"

Don then took over and stated his understanding of the gathering of the group. He served a summarizing and clarifying function while extending the initiation of the meeting begun by George. Keith then asked a question, "Have any of you been in such a group before?" Keith was seeking information. It was Jane Cotton who answered. She had been in a "spiritual search group" in another city and explained how that group had functioned. She provided information—another function needed in the group.

If leadership can be thought of as a series of needed functions, then George, Don, Keith, and Jane all in turn provided leadership. Throughout the evening, as various leadership functions were needed—initiating, seeking information, giving information, clarifying, elaborating, testing for consensus, summarizing—some member of the group usually supplied the need. In that moment, he or she was leader. Don, the designated leader, provided some functions himself, but allowed the others to lead as well.

Group theorists speak of another type of function which all groups need in addition to the task functions described above. They describe the following as group-building and maintenance functions: encouraging, mediating conflicts, gatekeeping, standard-setting, and relieving tension. The gatekeeper is one who "opens the gate" for another member to speak by saying something like, "We haven't heard from Betty yet." The tension-reliever may throw in humor or divert the group away from a touchy point. These maintenance functions make it possible for the group to carry on its business.

In the functional leadership or shared leadership concept, any group member who provides one of these needed elements is sharing the leadership load. Why should Don or Keith try to fulfill all the needed functions of the group? In the first place, probably neither is capable of seeing all the needs. Secondly, when leadership is shared among the members of the group, research has shown that their personal investment is higher, morale is higher, and the group tends to accomplish more work toward its goals. Group members feel that their presence and contributions are more important, so they naturally feel more closely identified with the group.

It should be remembered, however, that so long as one member of the group feels that he should or could be *the leader,* shared leadership will probably not be possible. This dominating person may be the designated leader or someone else. When everyone in the group accepts the fact that no one person needs to emerge as top dog, then all can relax and accept the contributions of others without seeing them as competitors, and the group has reached interdependence. When lay persons and clergy alike begin to understand the power and meaning of this new conception of leadership, the potential of the local congregation will be more fully realized. We must first give up the idea that leadership resides in *a* person who is somehow qualified to do our reading, thinking, and praying for us. In *Church Meetings That Matter,* Philip Anderson includes a helpful discussion of shared leadership and the biblical image of the servant. He reminds us that Jesus spoke of himself as a servant and suggests that this is the proper image for the Christian. In the functional leadership concept, the leader is the one who serves the needs of the group. Similarly, Jesus provides an image of a leader who gives himself in service, rather than the big-shot image of leadership so common today.[2]

THE LEADERSHIP FLEXIBILITY CONCEPT

The idea of leadership flexibility is a crucial one for the person who works with various kinds of groups. The person with designated leadership responsibilities is confronted by a wide range of possible leader styles. He may adopt a highly authoritarian style, for example, in which he makes all decisions for the group, allow-

[2] Philadelphia–Boston: United Church Press, 1965, Chap. VI.

ing the members very little freedom. On the other hand, he may feel more comfortable using a very permissive style in which he allows the group to make all necessary decisions. The difficulty with many of us is that we tend to adopt one style and use it come hell or high water. We get into a rut and stay there, ignoring the fact that different situations call for differing styles.

Dr. Warren Schmidt, a leadership researcher, has identified five basic leadership styles and places them on a continuum as indicated by this helpful diagram.[3]

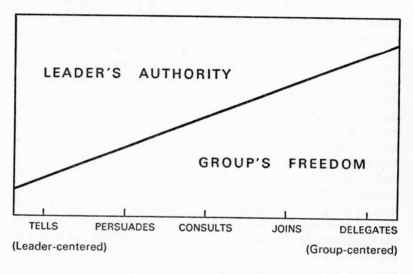

In the "telling" style, as the diagram suggests, the leader assumes most of the authority and leaves very little freedom to the group. This is the authoritarian stance, in which the leader assumes that he knows what is best for the group and tells the group how it is going to be.

When he moves to the "persuading" level, he still decides what is best for all, but sets out to persuade the group that his solution is what they need rather than simply telling them how it will be.

[3] *The Leader Looks at Styles of Leadership* (Leadership Resources, 1966), pp. 3–4.

He gives them some freedom—the freedom to say Yes or No to his decision.

At the "consulting" level the leader grants the group even more authority. He consults with them from the beginning. He may present a problem and ask them to suggest solutions. Or he may present his tentative solution and ask for their help in evaluating it. Then, after consulting the group, he makes his final decision on the basis of their wisdom.

At the "joining" level, the leader agrees to accept the decision of the group as they work on the problem together. He joins them as another member, participating in the decision but claiming no final wisdom or power of decision over the group solution.

Finally, at the opposite extreme from "telling" is "delegating." At this point, the leader simply turns the problem over to the group and asks them to solve it without him. He has delegated the problem to them completely and claims no further influence on the decision. In this style, as the diagram reveals, the group's freedom is almost complete and the leader's authority has decreased almost to the point of vanishing.

There is nothing sacred about the five styles mentioned, and other social scientists have offered more detailed analyses on the same continuum. The important point here is the concept of a possible variety of leadership styles as we work with groups of all sorts, from research teams to Bible-study groups. The question every leader must face is: "What is the appropriate style *now* for *this* group to do *this* job?" In addition, every leader must ask himself whether he tends to use the same style for every situation rather than operating on the principle of flexibility.

As Dr. Schmidt suggests, there are three main factors the leader must take into account as he decides on the appropriate leadership style. He must evaluate the forces within himself, within the group members, and in the situation.[4]

We have already seen in the case of Keith Thompson that personality factors do influence the leader's choice of style. Some persons, for a variety of internal reasons, tend to dominate and to feel more comfortable when they can make all the decisions for a

[4] *Ibid.,* pp. 5 ff.

group. Others feel more comfortable in the delegating style, where they never have to make a decision alone. Schmidt suggests that a man's value system is also an influence. Some leaders simply do not feel that others are equipped to make decisions for themselves, and assume that right for them. Similarly, a leader may have little or no confidence in the abilities of a particular group, and this feeling may influence his choice of style.

There are also forces in the group members which may influence the leader's choice of style. The group's readiness to assume responsibility is an important factor. If they are not emotionally ready to accept responsibility, even if technically or educationally equipped, this will influence the decision. The attitude of the group toward the task and their willingness to work on it will also be a factor.

Finally, there are forces in the situation which help determine the appropriate leadership style. Researchers became quite conscious of the role of situation in leadership during World War II. The typical illustration of the bomber crew makes this apparent. The bomber returning from a flight develops motor trouble and crashes in the jungle. While the plane was in the air, the pilot was in complete charge. However, he has had no jungle experience, and the gunnery sergeant is an expert in jungle survival. Here the situation calls for a shift in leadership from the pilot to the sergeant.

When we transfer the situational concept to a group situation, one factor to consider is the nature of the task. Is the task at hand too small to trouble the group with it? Does the leader consider the task too important to risk sharing it with the group? How effectively can this group work, and are they capable of dealing responsibly with the task at hand? All these may be thought of as situational questions.

Time pressure is also a realistic part of the situation. There are occasions when a crisis demands an immediate decision by the leader and he cannot realistically consult a group. When a child is drowning offshore, it is not time to call a committee meeting to decide who should rescue the child. It is time for an authoritarian decision.

As Schmidt reminds us, the long-range objectives of the organization may also influence the leader-style decision. If the organization has the growth and development of its members as a goal, this may suggest a leadership style which grants the group more responsibility. The same will be true if the development of teamwork and group morale is a goal.

It is possible to grant a group too much freedom and responsibility, creating anxiety and confusion. Most leaders tend to err in the opposite direction, however, and trust their groups too little. While a flexible style and an ability to evaluate the situation accurately are crucial qualities, church leaders are well advised to share leadership as much as possible. The fruits of shared leadership are more theologically consistent with the goals and purposes of a religious fellowship than are the results when a highly authoritarian style is used.

SOME LEADERSHIP PRINCIPLES

While shared leadership may be the most productive stance for most occasions, the flexibility concept reveals that firm leadership centered in one person is necessary at times. If I am asked to lead a one-hour discussion with a group of thirty people, I will not attempt to develop shared leadership. It is an impossibility with a group of thirty, and would only waste the hour for all of them. If I am asked to serve as chairman of a committee to plan a workshop for next year, it would be inappropriate to pull out and push the committee to develop shared leadership. At the same time, there are some basic principles which are in keeping with democratic leadership and with the Christian ethic.

The role of the group leader is parallel in many ways to that of a good parent, as I have already suggested. The leader needs to be sensitive to the possibility that his group may be ready to grow up and become independent of him. But even if the situation demands that he remain as "parent," the following general principles of good leadership may guide him in that role.

1. The group leader needs to communicate love and acceptance to his group just as a parent does to his child. He needs to say to his group in so many words, "This is a good group; you are acceptable." Groups tend to respond to praise and encourage-

ment like individuals. They can also become discouraged and develop inferiority feelings. I once worked with a very difficult group and at one point admitted to them, "This is one of the most difficult groups I have ever worked with." This remark, to my surprise, dampened the group's morale and effort was low for several days until they could tell me how it had affected them. They took the remark as rejection. Perhaps I could have been just as honest, but put it in a more constructive tone by saying, "I consider this group a real challenge—can you help me to understand you better?"

2. The loving parent also provides firm limits for his child. He cannot be afraid to say no. Similarly with the group leader. The group needs to sense the firmness of his authority. The leader must first accept himself as one with authority. He then needs to express that legitimate authority without apology or hesitation. This may well be one of the most crucial problems for all kinds of leaders—parents, ministers, teachers, foremen, and others. The group leader occasionally needs to say, "No, we don't deal with that." Or, "I'm sorry, but that's out of bounds."

3. He also needs to affirm the worth of individuals by his words and his actions.[5] It is often tempting to become so concerned with programs and business matters that the individual gets lost. But if the needs and motivations of the individual person are forgotten he may lose interest, become frustrated or angry, and end up blocking the task in one way or another. Programs exist for people, not people for programs.

4. Like a good parent, the group leader should help his group members to assume an increasing share of responsibility and leadership, to grow away from dependence upon him when the situation makes it appropriate. It is sometimes tempting to keep a group dependent upon oneself, just as it is tempting to keep a child dependent. It satisfies the dependency needs of the leader, but may prevent the growth of the group. Learning to let go is an important lesson of leadership.

5. The leader's job includes the responsibility to develop hon-

[5] I am indebted in this section to Gordon L. Lippitt for his article, "Ethical Dimensions of Group Leadership," *Pastoral Psychology* (March, 1967). The entire issue is on "Ministry Through Small Groups."

est, authentic fellowship in his group. For fellowship to develop, people need to know each other as well as the leader. Fellowship is a deep human need, and if people do not find their fellowship needs met they may lose interest. The creative, productive group is one in which there is a climate that permits the full play of ideas. The creative group tolerates a variety of behavior without sitting in judgment upon the individual because he is not conforming to a narrow code of thought or action.

7. The leader should create a climate in which group members can feel free to minister to each other. The danger lies in developing a group in which the leader meets all the important needs of persons. In theological language, this is developing the pastoral care role of the laity. We have mistakenly delegated pastoral care to the ordained clergy and lost the role of the whole church in this important ministry. The small group is one place we can recover that role for the laity.

8. The group leader has a responsibility to help the group evaluate its own behavior. Particularly when the group is struggling or having difficulty with its task, it may be helpful to pause for evaluation. A simple question can open the door: "We seem to be having difficulty; what do you think is really going on here?"

If we stand in the Judeo-Christian tradition, we must bring an ethical perspective to bear on our consideration of group leadership. As these eight dimensions imply, a tension must be maintained between the rights of the group and concern for the individual.

CHAPTER VI

THE INDIVIDUAL IN THE GROUP

The individual coming into a new group is faced with some crucial questions. They are important questions because they relate to basic life issues.[1] The individual must ask himself questions related to his acceptance or lack of acceptance in the group. He must ask himself questions about the role of power in the group. He must resolve the issue of intimacy or closeness, and he should raise questions around the problem of growth.

It may be helpful for you to ask yourself questions like these as you approach membership in a new group. Only you can answer the questions in these four areas of concern, for you alone know your needs and your capabilities.

As I now come to my first meeting with this group, do I belong? Am I really part of this group? Do I even want to be accepted by this group; do I want to be a part of what these people represent? Suppose I do want to be accepted. What must I do to be acceptable to them? How must I dress? Will they accept me if I wear some of the slouchy old clothes I enjoy wearing? Or if I wear some of the bright new ones? Or will they expect me to conform to some standard they have for the group?

[1] William C. Schutz has proposed that there are three basic interpersonal needs that all individuals have in common—the need for inclusion, the need for control, and the need for affection. See his *Firo: A Three-Dimensional Theory of Interpersonal Behavior* (New York: Basic Books, 1959).

What do I have to believe to be acceptable in this group? Will they try to change me? Will they try to force me into some kind of mold? I wonder if I would really be acceptable if I admitted some of my wild beliefs to them. And what about my behavior? Will I be expected to be "nice" and never disagree with anyone else in the group? Or on the other hand, will I feel pressured to tell dirty stories, or swear, or talk about sex and other personal matters? Will I be expected to discuss my personal problems in this group whether I want to or not?

Will I be able to join this group and reconcile this with my image of who I am, or will there be pressures to be somebody I'm not? In every group one must conform to some extent, and there is value in conforming for a common purpose. Without conformity, there would be no families, no churches, no nations. But will I be able to live with the degree of conformity this group expects without violating my sense of who I am?

And how will I feel if this group finds me unacceptable and rejects me? Or if I am too uncomfortable and decide to reject the group? How important is it to me to be included in this group? Could I live without this group? Could I really be me without them, considering the other groups I now belong to and which contribute to my identity? Are there enough other groups that *will* accept me?

The question of inclusion is crucial for us all. We cannot be individuals without belonging to some human groups. There is no such thing as an isolated individual. Research has shown that human beings require other human beings in order to remain sane. As some social scientists have put it: "To avoid complete personal disorganization man must conform to at least a minimal set of values required for participation in the groups to which he belongs."[2] So we ask ourselves which groups are most important to us and how much are we willing to pay to be included in them.

From infancy, when the family is our primary group, we are also asking the question of control.

Who is really in charge of this group? Is there one person who hands out the rewards and punishments? If so, do I want to line up

[2] Dorwin P. Cartwright and Ronald Lippitt, "Group Dynamics and the Individual," in *Group Development* (Washington, D.C.: National Education Association, 1961), p. 11.

with that person, or join the young dissidents who may be bucking his leadership? Is the chairman the one who has the power, or is it that quiet, confident person sitting quietly in the corner?

Can I take control of this group? Perhaps I'll test it and see. As I size up the other members, how do I rate? Am I strong enough to take the leadership and get away with it? Or could I control the group with one other person to help me? Can I team up with someone and take control? Or am I really more comfortable letting someone else call the shots while I exert a subtle influence on the sidelines? Would I really be comfortable being in control, even if I could take it? Do I need that much power to satisfy my ego?

And if I could take control, could I maintain it? Would I be acceptable to the group if I managed to take over, or would they reject me for being too dominant as a newcomer? Would they accept me as their leader but turn away from me as a friend? Which is more important to me? Will this group respect me as a person and give me some share in controlling the decisions of the group? Or will I have to earn that right in time? What are the avenues to power in this group? Right behavior? Right belief? Faithful attendance? How important is it to me to attain that power?

Many people can admit that inclusion or acceptance is one of their basic life questions, but some have more difficulty in admitting that they have any aspirations to power and control. They find it harder to let the control questions into their awareness, but their concern with power may be revealed through manipulative behavior and leadership struggles.

At some level of our consciousness, we are also asking ourselves questions in the area of intimacy.

How close do I really want to be to these people? Would I like to be very close, sharing deeply of who I am? Or do I need more distance from people to be comfortable? Do I trust this group enough to allow them close?

How close do they want me to be? For that matter, how close are they to each other? Am I as close as everyone else, or am I a special case? Will this be a group which provides enough warmth to satisfy my needs for intimacy with others? Or will there be more intimacy than I can tolerate? How much closeness am I comfortable with before I begin pulling away from people? Is this a group which just talks, or do people also touch each other? Or kiss each other? Am I threatened by people who touch or hug each other freely? Can I kiss and be kissed by friends without misreading the intent? Am I able to communicate my acceptance of them in tangible ways so they know I care about them?

In addition to asking ourselves these basic human questions of inclusion, control, and affection we sometimes ask the question of growth, particularly in groups organized for an educational or therapeutic purpose.

Do I want to grow? Really? Do I want to grow if it means changing something in myself? Or am I basically satisfied with who I am? Wouldn't I rather stay as I am?

Do I want to grow badly enough to open myself to the influence of these people in this group? Don't I really know more than they do anyway? Should I listen to what they have to say to me? Should I risk the possibility that I may hear something painful—something I don't want to hear about myself? Wouldn't it be easier and safer just to go on hiding behind my mask? And could I trust them if I take the mask off? Will they treat me with kindness and gentleness? Or might they destroy me?

After all, why should I risk my image with these people? Isn't it a satisfactory image? What they don't know won't hurt them. On the other hand, they see things about me which I can't see. They see *me* —in ways I do not. Do I want to know what they see? Can I take it? Can I profit from it, or will I be crushed by it? How badly do I want to know who I am? How badly do I want to grow, and what price am I willing to pay?

And so we as individuals ponder the extent of our involvement and our investment in the various groups to which we belong. Our needs vary from time to time, and the ability of the group to fulfill our needs varies as well. And so we move in and pull back, we expose ourselves and then we hide, we bid for leadership and then we submit to another.

There is no person who does not need to belong to some groups in order to survive as a person. Who and what he will be to those groups he decides every day.

CHAPTER VII

COMMON GROUP PROBLEMS

The ten filed silently into the doctor's office and took chairs. A nurse nodded and disappeared into an inner corridor. Several members of the group began reading voraciously in the three-year-old copies of *Today's Health,* while others sat staring off dejectedly into space. After an hour or two, a door suddenly opened and the doctor appeared.

"Sorry to keep you waiting. I'm a little behind schedule today," he said smiling.

"Oh, it's perfectly all right, doctor," the group mumbled almost in unison.

"Will you come into my office, please?" The group followed silently as the doctor led the way down the hall into a large office.

"Please take a chair," said the doctor, pointing to a circle of ten chairs in the middle of the room. "Now what seems to be the trouble?"

"We seem to have a communication blockage," Bob replied, "between the perception apparatus and the transmission device."

"Oh, no, that's not it," cried Irene. "We have a leadership clique problem, and . . . ." She was interrupted by Gloria.

"No, no, we simply have an overload of hostility, and the system won't . . . ." By that time the entire group had gotten to their feet. They were all waving their arms trying to get the floor.

"Wait a minute," said the doctor. "Let's cool it. Just stand quietly while I make some tests." He then took out an instrument something like a stethoscope and went slowly around the circle listening to each member in turn with his instrument. He then took small wooden paddles and had each member of the group open his mouth while he looked inside. After several other routine tests, the doctor seemed satisfied.

"Ah, yes," he said at last. "This group is suffering from a simple case of group depression heightened by an inadequate self-image and a slight case of the common group cold." The group members breathed sighs of relief and looked at each other smiling and nodding. "Now if you will just have this prescription filled, and take one of these tablets before each group meeting, this should all clear up in a month or two."

If only group problems could be solved by taking a few pills! If only we had doctors who could prescribe the answers to problems like racial conflict, political corruption, and international tension. In point of fact, we do have an emerging corps of human relations specialists who can diagnose group and intergroup problems and propose solutions. Too often, like the person who needs his illness, we choose not to listen to the solutions and dismiss them for our own home remedies.

There are some common group problems which can be identified. While there may not be pills which will cause them to vanish, there may be some suggested directions toward answers. Many group problems have already been referred to in this book. There are problems which grow out of conflicts in expectations about the group, differences in understanding of the contract, leadership competition, and relation to authority. In this chapter, I shall try to isolate a few of the more common group problems not yet treated.

It is amusing to ponder some of the "illnesses" that afflict groups and their parallels in the diseases of human individuals. There may be such a thing as the common group cold, complete with headaches, a certain amount of stuffiness, and insensitivity to others. There may be several varieties of group flu, a disabling affliction with a variety of nasty symptoms which will go away after a while. There may be a parallel to the mumps among individuals who experience a swelling of the voice box and an inability to talk when their feelings have been hurt or the group isn't going their way. Groups may also suffer mysterious malignancies which prove fatal

at times unless dealt with promptly. While these tongue-in-cheek
examples may not be altogether helpful, they will serve to remind
us that groups have problems and ailments which have some pre-
dictable symptoms, can be diagnosed, and may often be cured. I
shall use three disguised case examples from my own experience
to illustrate some common group illnesses.

Case 1.   The Dominator

I once worked with a group of twelve men and women whose purpose as a group was to discuss their common concerns as church
leaders. One man, whom I shall call Clarence, tended to make
long speeches whenever he talked. He didn't appear to hear the
others when they spoke, but delivered long monologues which
usually bored the rest. He would repeat himself, adding unnecessary details to his story, and drone on and on, seemingly unable
to stop himself. As someone put it, Clarence had no terminal
facilities. His lack of consideration was revealed when one member attempted to interrupt him after he had been speaking for about
five minutes.

"Could I say something?" said Tim in a firm but courteous tone.

"In just a minute when I'm through," replied Clarence, continuing his monologue with hardly a pause. A few minutes later,
someone again tried to break through Clarence's speech, but to
no avail.

Another crucial factor in this case was the personal difficulty
Clarence revealed to the group. Apparently he had a pattern of
poor relationships in his job situation and was in danger of being
fired. The other members of the group were quite aware of his
difficulty and sensed a deep-seated weakness underneath the ver-
bosity. The result was that, while the group became increasingly
angry at Clarence, it did not seem appropriate to attack him with
the anger his behavior deserved. They feared that he "couldn't
take it" and would break down or fly into a rage. On a number of
occasions when a member of the group or I would attempt to help
him see what he was doing, he would turn on us rather than accept
the criticism as valid. As I interpret what happened, Clarence's
weakness and vulnerability caused the group to deny its anger for

him and drive it underground. That is to say, the anger was repressed or held inside.

The Problem of Apathy

The next development was the appearance of apathy. The discussion became sluggish, and members had difficulty in agreeing on what to discuss. Furthermore, discussion was on a superficial level. No one seemed willing to invest much in the group or to risk revealing much of himself. The trust level was very low. As a result, there was little sharing in depth. The group was testy and tended to find itself in conflict rather easily. However, in spite of the conditions I have described, some work was done and the group was helpful to some members. Another symptom of the group's difficulty was the tendency of members to blame me for their inability to function smoothly. As I understood this scapegoating trend, they could not express their anger openly to Clarence (or did not dare), so it was displaced onto the leader. The practice of scapegoating the leader is a fairly common group phenomenon, particularly when the group has difficulty in focusing its irritation on the appropriate target.

One approach to group problems would be to describe this as a group with problems of apathy or low involvement of its members, or one which has difficulty in making decisions about its agenda. This seems to me to be attacking matters at the wrong level. A more total approach reveals that the apathy, low investment, and difficulties in discussion are symptoms of a deeper problem: how to deal with Clarence.

This group had to make a very difficult decision. They had to decide, on an unspoken level, whether to confront Clarence with their real anger at his behavior or to deny the anger in order to protect him. After making a few unsuccessful attempts, they chose not to confront him. As a result, the group never did really fulfill its potential.

We are left with some questions. Was protecting Clarence worth the cost to the group? Should he be permitted to foul up group after group without ever fully facing the consequences of his behavior? Would it be all loss if Clarence were actually to break down and require therapy to face himself and reconstruct his approach to people? This is a tremendously important question, with deep ethical implications. In spite of the cost to themselves, I am not sure the group made the wrong decision in dealing with Clarence. There are no easy answers to such questions.

It is very common for an individual to attempt to dominate a group. While the behavior may not be as extreme as in this case, many of the same symptoms may be present. The group may be afraid to interrupt him, or fear his anger if they oppose him. And so they let him get away with running the show, doing most of the talking and making most of the decisions. In the meantime, the group members become more and more angry. In church groups particularly, it is often considered wrong to express anger openly. So it is veiled or denied and goes underground to plague the group in other insidious ways.

Dealing with the Dominator

There is only one way to deal with the dominator in a group. That is to tell him openly how you feel about his behavior, how it affects you. You are not judging him; you do not need to know why he behaves the way he does. You simply share honestly with him how his behavior affects *you*. The sooner this can be done the better. The longer he is allowed to dominate, the farther underground the hostility is driven and the more damaging it can be to personal, family, and community relations. For hostility must go somewhere. If it is denied, it will reappear in often surprising and violent guise. When a group or individual cannot find the simple courage to face a man like Clarence and tell him how it is, they may expect increasingly difficult communication in that group.

The individual who does not feel he can trust his own feelings enough to risk them in the group will not grow until he does. You explore the validity of your feelings by testing them with other group members and calling out their honesty. On occasion a group may fear to be honest, and members may even deny that they, too, are angry with the dominator. It sometimes helps to test one's feelings privately with another group member for re-assurance.

There are other reasons for apathy in groups, less complex than the repressed anger operating in Clarence's case. Groups may become apathetic if they feel the subject they are discussing is not important or that they have an unimportant task. Or members may become apathetic if they feel the task is important, but they do not have the resources or ability to deal with it. A sense of helplessness may result. In such a case, calling attention to the apathy may not help the group to change, but a discussion of why it feels helpless may lead to a new perspective.

Case 2.   Superficiality and Frustration

A number of ministers attended a two-day retreat in which I was their small-group leader. From the beginning, this group had difficulty sharing in any depth. The discussion tended to remain on a superficial level. They spoke of ways to improve attendance on Sunday mornings, an interesting youth rally someone had attended, and other objective and external matters. These might not have been considered superficial if our contract had been for discussion of minor parish concerns. But rather, it called for the sharing of deeper personal and professional experiences.

When I suggested that we talk about why the group was having difficulty, one problem emerged with some clarity. A minister whom I shall call Fred took the occasion to ask, "What are your credentials to work with groups, anyway? Are you a psychologist or what?" As we talked out his concern, Fred showed deep-seated fears about being "opened up" or revealed in some frightening way, and he challenged me as his way of announcing that he did not trust me or the group. He did not really want to know what my credentials were; he dismissed them as though they did not exist. If I had been Sigmund Freud he would not have been impressed, for he would not have felt any more secure about himself.

As a result, Fred communicated his reservations to others between sessions and in nonverbal ways while in the group. He held back visibly, sitting farther away than other members, looking uninterested, and scoffing at my efforts as a leader. Fred also let the group know that he himself had credentials which made him knowledgeable in group psychology and caused him to distrust me by comparison. One of his underlying reasons for attacking me may have been the desire to become leader himself. This ploy is often seen in groups. If one can demolish the leader by under-cutting his authority in some way, then the way is open to take over. I remember the minister who took me to task on one occa-sion for using a rather strong slang expression, then assumed that this made him the moral leader of the group. He had not stooped to use "uncouth" language and felt he had disqualified me by pointing out my Achilles' heel.

In Fred's case, the group did not share his reservations. They tried to hear him out and understand him, but he resisted sharing very deeply of himself. His attacks on me made me angry, and I had to be honest with him about this. The open facing of Fred's behavior by the group helped to ease the situation, but we never convinced him that he could trust us. He imported his problem into the group, and in the short time together we did not help him to deal with it.

The Avoidance of Depth

Another member of that same group—Dean—worked very hard to keep the discussion on a superficial level. He simply re-fused to say anything about himself, and his contributions were all calculated to conceal him from the group. Others tried to tell him that they wanted to know him as a person, but he managed to evade the point of their comments. He finally admitted that he did not believe in groups or intend to participate. In fact, he said, if he had known he was going to find himself in a small group he would not have come (he never did explain why he had come, in light of the invitation which was quite clear as to the nature of the conference).

Dean went further. He was determined not to be one of us, and did his best to undermine the group for everyone else; he not only did not want to be in a group, but did not want anyone else to be in a group either. The group was able to help him a little to see that he had a deep need to avoid closeness and that he also tried to keep others from experiencing it. Dean did not change his behavior, but he was pushed to an awareness of what he was doing.

Men like Fred and Dean appear in groups with some regularity. They do not feel comfortable in small groups where people become known in some depth. Rather than avoid such experiences altogether, they prefer to spoil them for others. Their need to control the situation is a major source of difficulty, and the result in this case was a fairly superficial level of interaction and a growing sense of frustration in the group. If the group had not leveled with Fred and Dean, the frustration would have been much worse.

Leveling with people like these two men, uncomfortable as it may be, is the only way to solve a problem like this. It does not guarantee a satisfactory solution, but at least it permits everyone the opportunity to express how he feels about it and helps clear the air. When a group does not have the strength or courage to discuss openly the manipulative behavior of men like Fred and Dean, it is in for trouble.

Case 3.   The Missing Father Figure

This case illustrates the importance of the authority figure and the dynamics that surround him. About twenty men were attending a ten-day workshop. There were three leaders: a director and two associates. On the sixth day of the workshop, the director was called away and had to leave the group in charge of the two younger men, who met with the group the next morning to carry on the program for the day. The group was scheduled to attend an early worship service at a nearby church and return for a discussion of the experience.

When the service ended, a strange thing happened. The group seemed unwilling to leave and return for the scheduled discussion. They lingered at the coffee hour and would not leave even when the conference leaders circulated through the crowd and asked them to start for their cars. Several members of the group vanished and did not return for the discussion at all, while others drifted in casually for the next half hour. When the puzzled leaders asked why they were late for the discussion, they replied, "What discussion?" They appeared honestly puzzled at being expected to return. No one seemed to be able to recall the announcement the day before describing the program for the day in detail.

Several facts seem clear. (1) The director did leave on Saturday. (2) The program was announced to the group in detail on Saturday, yet *not one man* remembered it. (3) The group's behavior on Sunday was very unusual. I am convinced that this event is understandable only in light of authority dynamics. The director represents an authority figure in such a group and is a fatherlike figure on a deep subconscious level. Age is no factor here; the director could be younger than all the group members, yet still be seen as a father figure. When "father" left, there may have been some feelings of having been deserted. There were probably feelings of anger at his leaving, just as a young child feels angry with his father for going out of town on a business trip. The child expresses the anger in rebellious behavior, wetting the bed while his father is away, or being punished at school, or poking a neighbor kid in the eye. Groups can express rebellious behavior of the same sort without any conscious awareness *in any member's mind!*

Unconscious Group Decisions

Rebellious behavior and the group's anger may have been expressed on Sunday morning when they "forgot" to return for their scheduled discussion. The failure to return may well have been an example of an important phenomenon: an *unconscious group decision*. Groups often "decide" on a particular course of action without the decision ever consciously occurring to any one person in the group. For example, I am convinced that church groups often make unconscious and unspoken group decisions to level off at a safe, superficial level of interaction which will not threaten anyone too much. This is the "do not rock the boat" syndrome, and honest recognition of this all-too-human tendency may be a necessary prelude to change.[1] If the unconscious group decision is a human possibility, it may help to explain much of the contra-

[1] A more detailed discussion of this tendency of groups to make unconscious decisions and its effect on church life may be found in my book, *The God-Evaders* (New York: Harper & Row, 1966).

dictory behavior of groups like churches which verbalize a purpose but never reach the stage of acting on their resolutions.

In the case of the missing father figure, the two remaining leaders were faced with a decision. They could either ignore the rebellious behavior and proceed with the scheduled program, or they could attempt to resolve the feelings in some way. They chose the latter course. At the next scheduled meeting of the group, they embarked on an exploration of the group's unusual behavior. A heated discussion followed. Few members of the group felt that there was any connection with their "failure" to return for the discussion and the director's exit from the conference. However, they did express strong, angry feelings out of proportion to the magnitude of the issue under discussion. No logical explanations were ever agreed upon, but the mood of the group changed visibly as they were given an opportunity to vent their feelings. Perhaps these were feelings of anger and rejection at the director's "abandonment" of them. That would be my guess, though we will never know with any certainty. The conference proceeded on a creative and fruitful level of encounter and no further "rebellious" behavior occurred.

A few general observations may be made. In any group situation, large or small, there are probably some deep authority dynamics involved beneath the surface. Unless it is functioning smoothly as an interdependent peer group, in which all share the leadership to some extent, the group probably regards someone in it—consciously or unconsciously—as a father or authority figure. The designated group leader, the senior minister, the director of religious education, or some honored individual may be the person to whom they look for direction and guidance. If the signals coming from the father figure are positive and approving, the group will probably be pleased. If the signals are angry, disapproving, or cold, the group may be affected in a negative way without ever being consciously aware of the source of the difficulty.

At the same time, groups often express *resistance* to authority figures comparable to the resistance noted in therapy patients toward their therapists or psychiatrists. Therapy groups occasionally develop massive group resistance and refuse to engage in their "work" of discussing personal problems. Some small-group behavior may be understood as resistance to an authority figure. This authority may be present in the group as a designated leader or a leading member, or may not be within the group at all.

SOME MISCELLANEOUS GROUP PROBLEMS

It may be well to outline, in less detail, a few additional group problems that arise with some regularity.

1. Groups can occasionally be hurtful. I have been deeply impressed with how often they are helpful and sensitive and understanding, and how rarely they are hurtful and insensitive and rejecting. However, it is possible for groups, like people, to be self-centered or angry or immature. On occasion, a group will become too clinical, probing an individual's motivation and making him feel like an amoeba under a microscope or a piece of fat in the frying pan. At times like these, a group can be hurtful. I have also seen a group of sensitive people ignore the tears of a person in distress, perhaps out of embarrassment. But it is more common to see a group member reach out a hand, put an arm around the shoulder, or offer a handkerchief to the hurt member.

If a group is acting in a hurtful way, and there is a designated leader, it is his responsibility to establish clear limits for the group. "I'm sorry, but that's out of bounds. We don't probe another person's personal history!" Said in a firm way, this kind of comment can go a long way toward preventing further pain. If there is no established leader, any group member should feel it his right and responsibility to raise the issue for discussion. He might say, "I feel we have moved too far in a clinical direction and are in danger of probing too deeply. Does anyone else feel that way?"

Groups can also have the opposite problem, being superficial, or probing too little. In either case, an understanding that there will be regular evaluation of the group's process behavior will help open the door for a critical appraisal of such issues.

2. It is also possible for a group to be warm, concerned, and sensitive but completely self-centered. It may have such a warm fellowship that it becomes turned in upon itself with no awareness or concern for the outside world and its problems. As I indicated

in another chapter, groups sometimes move through phases of self-centeredness, but when they remain caught there for long periods of time it may not be a healthy growth situation for anyone. Again in this instance, if regular evaluation is built into the structure from the beginning, it will be much more difficult for the group to evade its shortcomings.

It is also a sign of realism for people to admit that there are times when groups have served their usefulness or fulfilled their purpose and should die. Church groups are famous for continuing long after their usefulness has ended. They just go on, like Old Man River, rolling along because they always have, with no clear purpose or direction. When a group becomes centered on itself, this may be one indication that its usefulness has ceased.

3. A common problem in groups is the existence of a small power clique. This subgroup meets in between stated meetings of the group and makes decisions that affect the whole group. They railroad decisions through the meetings before the "outsiders" in the group know what has hit them, creating anger and resistance. They often do not listen to the views of others outside their clique, further frustrating the group. The open confrontation of such a group is the only way to deal with their tactics, unless the group splits into two opposing power cliques. This tends to harden the lines of conflict rather than freeing the group's creative potential.

4. I once met with a group of professional people for an encounter experience in a most inappropriate setting. The room to which we were assigned was designed as a chapel. An altar and trappings were dimly concealed at one end of the room. The chairs were hard metal, and the cold tile floor did not invite informal sprawling. This discrepancy between the purpose of a meeting and the setting is a common problem. So many church buildings are constructed as formal settings that they do not encourage the kind of personal, informal encounter we now feel is essential for religious growth. This conflict simply calls for us to be aware of the setting we choose for a particular type of meeting, especially for small-group meetings. To hold such a meeting in the first three pews of a large, dark, wood-paneled sanctuary is hardly encouraging to open discussion or personal sharing. This factor should

also have some impact on church planners as they design the buildings that will contain or encourage our religious expression of the future.

5. It is probably a fact that groups fail when they do not meet the needs of their members. The difficulty is that people often fear to share what their real needs are, giving the group no chance to meet them. There are also times when people really do not know their own needs, so cannot verbalize them. When honest sharing is possible, a group will have a far better chance to serve the deeper concerns of its members.

6. As the Clarence case indicated, groups often run into deep problems of relationships between members. Such problems can immobilize them. There are times when the sexual dynamics in a group become too intense and tend to dominate the interaction. A strong, motherly woman can tie a group to her as the "group mother," with the male members competing for her attention in an effort to be the "favorite son." This is not necessarily bad, unless it becomes the dominant interaction and the group task is avoided or lost sight of.

Similarly, I have seen an attractive girl tie a group up by seducing the group and becoming its "sweetheart." In this case, the men may be competing for her favors and forget their primary purpose as a group. And beware the jilted suitors in a group when she chooses a favorite! It is possible to have a "group father," a "group mother," and a "group sweetheart" all in the same group, somewhat complicating the dynamics. I suggest these possibilities, which are very real, in order to point out that there can be deep underlying relationship problems in any group. There are times when these are so complex and personal that it is not feasible to discuss them openly in the group. It is a sign of a healthy group when it can openly acknowledge some of these problems and try to work them through.

In all these group problems, there is nothing like the openness and honest sharing of feelings as a general prescription for group health. This honesty has a price. It may be painful. But pain is often the necessary prelude to health.

CHAPTER VIII

NONVERBAL AND EXPERIMENTAL GROUP METHODS

Imagine yourself arriving at a retreat center for a weekend conference on "Nonverbal and Experimental Group Methods." To your surprise, at the first session you are asked to sit on the rug and take off your shoes and stockings. Then you are instructed to line up with the other twenty people in your group and take the hand of the person in front of you and the person behind you. You may not talk. The group then proceeds out the door onto the terrace. You notice immediately the various sensations coming to you through your feet. First the warm pavement of the terrace, then the rough gravel of the path, relieved by the cool softness of the grass. It occurs to you how good it feels to walk around barefoot. Your feet are encased in shoes so much of the time that you had forgotten what it was like to have sensations through your feet. After all, there are people all over the world who have never owned shoes, and you sense a feeling of identification with the shoeless poor.

Then you find yourself slowly becoming aware of something else. As your feet contact the ground, you feel support there. You let the muscles of your feet relax a bit so you are no longer resisting contact with the earth. Support! Strong support. And that sup-

105

port has been there all the time, offering itself if only you can accept it and cooperate with it. You feel a little stronger somehow, as though you have found a new ally you never knew you had.

You become conscious that the woman ahead of you has a warm, firm grip which seems to communicate a seriousness of purpose, yet a relaxed acceptance of things as they are. It makes you aware of the fact that you are tense, tight, and probably communicating your tightness through your hands. The man behind you, by contrast, is ill at ease if you can judge by his sweating palms. He seems nervous, as if this experience might harm him in some way. There is no warmth in his grip, which seems only to tolerate your hand rather than grasping it. You hadn't realized how much people communicate through their hands.

You also notice how vivid the colors of the flowers appear. The intensity of their beauty just hadn't struck you with such force in a long time. You notice that some people in the line occasionally reach out and touch the pine needles or the softness of a leaf. You try to recall the instructions, but you remember no prohibitions about touching. The leader then leads the line in a loop, so that each person passes slowly in front of each other person and looks into his or her face. The faces are so different. They say so much. They say, "I like myself," or "I like people." Some faces say, "Don't look at me and I won't look at you." You make mental notes about some faces you would like to know better and some that bother you.

THE SHARING OF FEELINGS

A short time later, the group is back inside sitting on the rug in a large circle. You are talking about what you felt and experienced. One woman mentions the various noises she heard on her walk. You realize that you didn't even notice sounds. Why not? Another person was impressed by the smells in the garden, while others did not use their sense of smell at all. The man with the sweaty palms talks about his sense of embarrassment at walking around barefoot. "I felt like some kind of a kook," he confesses. He admits that he felt foolish the whole time and really didn't appreciate the various sensations coming to him. Others indicate that they felt a little self-conscious at first, but then began to relax and enjoy the experience.

You become aware of the fact that you are now more sensitive to your environment than usual. Your powers of observation are sharpened, and you are more aware of your self as including not only a mind but a body. You realize that your body is sending you signals constantly, signals usually ignored or blunted by a narrow focus of attention. You are also dimly aware of a growing sense of identification with this group of people, many of whom have expressed feelings similar to your own.

The leader reminds the group that you have just been through an experimental nonverbal exercise designed to heighten awareness of one's world. "This is part of a whole new thrust in our culture," he explains. "We are becoming increasingly aware of the fact that the person is a whole being with mind, body, and feelings. We can no longer ignore the body and appeal only to the intellect if we want to communicate with people. The religious life must not be a sterile, intellectualized process, but a vital, vibrant recognition that God has given us bodies as well. We will now proceed with some experiences designed to bring us into contact with other individuals as whole persons." You make a mental note that this simple exercise might well be used with several groups when you get back home.

NONVERBAL COMMUNICATION

The leader then instructs you to stand up and move about the room introducing yourselves to each other. He also stipulates several rules for this exercise: "You are not allowed to shake hands, and you are not allowed to talk. You must find new ways of making yourselves known to each other." Your first impulse is one of panic. "How can I possibly communicate who I am if I can't speak?" You wonder if this might not be a convenient time to slip out and wash your hands, but you decide to stick it out and see what happens. The leader turns on a phonograph, and some lively music fills the room. A young woman with a friendly smile is standing before you. The moment of truth has arrived.

You suddenly realize that the smile is saying a great deal. You can't help but smile in return, and communication has begun. You point to her brightly colored blouse and indicate by gestures and smiles that you like her choice. She beams in return and touches your arm, gripping it slightly, then moves on. A man appears before you in a turtle-neck shirt, and you clutch your neck, point to his shirt, and grin appreciatively. You notice that some people are responding to the music by moving rhythmically, and two people have linked arms and are dancing around, laughing and smiling. Two of the men have begun wrestling each other around, though it seems to be in good fun. It occurs to you that you have remained rooted in one spot, while others seem more free to move about and introduce themselves to each other. You wish you felt more free to respond to the music and move about.

You are then instructed to locate a partner with whom you will spend some time during the conference. You look hurriedly around, feeling very self-conscious. There was one interesting fellow you thought you might like. But then there's that attractive young girl with the bright blouse, but perhaps it would be too obvious if you chose her—and someone has just grabbed her off, anyway. Most of the people are already paired off, and you begin to wonder why you are so slow when a face appears before you and the decision is taken out of your hands.

The leader shows you how to face your new partner, reach your hands out and touch fingertips. The two of you are then to explore the space between you by moving your hands in unison, pushing, yielding, testing, responding. Together you develop some patterns of rhythm, and you begin to relax and enjoy the encounter. After a minute or two of exploring, you and your partner are instructed to talk together about how you felt during the exercise.

"One thing I noticed," says your new friend, "—you seemed very tentative at first but gained confidence as you went along."

"Yes, I think you're right," is your reply. Your acquaintance has begun at a level of sharing and identifying feelings.

EYEBALL TO EYEBALL

After a few minutes of conversation, you are interrupted again by the leader. "Now stand and look your partner squarely in the eye for as long as you can. Just see what you can see in his face." You find the assignment more difficult than it sounds. You find yourself feeling very self-conscious and you look away repeatedly, but gradually the smiles around your partner's eyes invite you to look more deeply. You become aware of the genuine warmth in his face, and you decide you will like getting to know this man. You think you also see some pain in his eyes, and you wonder what may have hurt him so deeply. At the same time his eyes are steady and clear, and you get a feeling of strength from his face. In the discussion moments that follow you share some of these feelings with your partner, and you are surprised to discover that your instincts were basically sound, your interpretations accurate. You gain a new confidence in your own judgment. He seems to have you pretty well pegged, too, as he shares some insights that surprise you.

In the next phase of the session, you and your partner are instructed to locate two others with whom you would like to be in a group. This time you decide to try some new behavior and act more swiftly. "How about that interesting girl with the bright blouse?" you ask. Your partner nods his agreement and you are already moving in her direction. You end up in groups of six, and you are pleased to note the balance in the group.

Your group then teams up with another group of six, and you sit in a small circle with five others while your partner is sitting in the outside circle observing you. He sits so that he can see your face. The six in the outside circle are then instructed to cover their ears and look only for nonverbal behavior cues. Your own inner circle is told to spend fifteen minutes in conversation "getting acquainted."

A sandy-haired young man begins, "Well, I guess somebody has to break the ice, so here goes. I was born in Peoria, Illinois, and . . . ." The young man goes on and on, offering details about his life in Peoria while the others fidget.

After about five minutes, you volunteer, "Maybe we'd better move on, or we won't have time . . . ." You hope the sandy-haired young man's partner will clue him in on how long he monopolized the group. After the fifteen-minute conversation you and your partner huddle in a corner for five minutes, and he tells you what he observed about your behavior in the inner circle. You hadn't realized that you were tapping your foot nervously while the young man spoke, nor that your face revealed your impatience.

Your partner then takes his place in the inner circle and you observe him. In a second round, you are back in the inner circle and your partner both looks and listens, while you close your eyes as you talk. This time you are instructed to share an experience from your early life which has helped to make you the person you are. Afterward you realize that you know the other five in your circle far better from sharing that one life experience than you did from all the personal facts they had offered as credentials in the first round. You also realize how much more carefully you were listening with your eyes closed, but how much data you did not have that comes through the person's face and eyes and gestures. You make a note to try this simple structured exercise in your teacher-training program when you get home.

You then enlarge the circle and sit in your group of twelve to discuss how you feel about the entire exercise. You become aware of a deep feeling of identification with these eleven people, and you are glad to be a part of this group. You can now look forward to spending the weekend with some people you like and have already come to know in some depth. One man in the circle comments, "Why, I already feel I know some of you better than people I've known for ten years."

Another notes that he feels more aware of what people communicate through their faces, and how he uses his own face to communicate his feelings.

"I've never paid much attention to my feelings before," says another, "and I now see that it's a pretty important part of communication."

Your mind flashes back to some of the weekend conferences you have attended. You can recall sitting in a large circle that first evening, with each person telling a little about himself. "I'm John Dear, and I live in George, Washington. I'm a civil engineer with the Weebuildem Corporation. I'm married and have five children, Betty Lou, Jimmy . . . ." You wonder at the fact that an entire weekend of listening to speeches and talking with people left you not knowing them much better than before, while you already have a deep bond with this group in a few hours.

THE PERSON AS A UNITY

Next morning in theory session, the leader is explaining. "In our culture, we have become too intellectualized. We have cut ourselves off from our feelings and tended to deny them. We are embarrassed by feelings and don't really know how to deal with them. Similarly, we are ashamed of our bodies. We prefer to pretend we don't have bodies, and so we do not listen to what our bodies are telling us."

One serious young man interrupts with a question. "Is this why our religion has become so much a matter of right doctrines? Have we intellectualized our faith and made it into a set of sterile intellectual propositions?"

The leader smiles. "You'd have to answer that for yourself. I think it is very possible that we've overemphasized doctrines. We tend to cut people off who don't state their faith in the same intellectual categories we do. We're moving away from that emphasis now, thank goodness. I'd like to make another point. There is an exciting new breakthrough coming now in our awareness of the connection between the body and the mind. For example, there are new forms of therapy that work on the level of physical movement and cut through to deeper levels of the mind much faster than talking."

Your partner from the night before has his hand up. "Can you give us an example?"

"Yes," replies the leader. "A man named Albert Pesso has developed a new therapy approach called psychomotor therapy growing out of his work as an instructor of dance. Pesso discovered that many of his dance pupils had physical barriers which prevented them from becoming really good dancers. These bodily barriers, he discovered, were actually messages about inner states of feeling. By working with movement therapy methods, he is able to help people discover these barriers and work them out in a relatively short time. Some of the problems that emerge require long-term therapy, but many people experience a breakthrough with this approach. Some of them may have verbalized their problems for years without solving them. It's really a very exciting new development, and psychiatrists and analysts now come to Mr. Pesso regularly to learn this method, as an adjunct to their other approaches."

"What is an example of a bodily message and how would Pesso approach it?" you ask a bit skeptically.

"Well, take this example. When he conducts a workshop, Al Pesso has the group stand in a relaxed stance which he has devised. He suggests that you 'listen' to your body by asking yourself where you are tense. Some people report that they are tense in the neck or that their legs ache. Pesso has developed a sensitivity to what these 'messages' mean, and he works with the individual to help him find a way to work out the tenseness physically. He may suggest that it sounds like a problem of hostility, and then he may help the individual to act out his rage by pounding pillows, or yelling. The key is that the therapy centers on action rather than just talking about the rage. The individual may also talk out his intellectual associations with the feelings, but the emphasis is on movement as an avenue to health."

The leader continues, "Another way Pesso helps the individual deal with feelings is through accommodation. One person physically strikes out in the direction of another as though hitting him. The accommodating partner remains just out of reach, but accommodates by yelling and recoiling as though struck. He may scream and fall to the floor, giving the striker satisfaction in the expression of his anger without actually harming anyone. Some married couples have found this an excellent way to deal with some of their deep feelings of rage so they can communicate with each other more rationally again."

He goes on, "Pesso has also helped many people work through their father-mother hangups by what he calls structuring. When a person's behavior suggests that he has problems in the area of his early attachment to his mother (or to father in the woman's case), Pesso helps structure a normal family. He has someone represent a negative mother with all her bad characteristics, while another stands in for the negative father. Two others play the role of positive mother and positive father. This helps the individual express his legitimate or exaggerated anger toward the negative figures, driving them away, while the positive figures remain. He is then helped to work through his feelings toward these parental figures through movement. This sometimes clears up deep feelings which have been fouling up communication for years. The oedipal conflicts are often so deeply buried that verbalizing fails to get at them."

You push your question further. "You wouldn't suggest that we try this without special training?"

"Oh, certainly not. Psychomotor therapy should be attempted only by a *therapist* with special training. I simply mention it as an example of some of the exciting new developments, and there are many others in addition to Albert Pesso who are making discoveries in this direction. However, there are some helpful ways we can use this important connection between physical movement and health. We can build educational and growth experiences such as the walk through the garden last night. This helps us to come into communication with our feelings and with each other through movement and words. We used to rely upon words alone, and that was rather sterile."

Another hand is up. "What does this have to say about worship in most of our churches today? Most worship consists of verbalization."

The leader thinks a moment, then replies, "I'm certain there are deep implications for our approach to worship, and we may be on the verge of some major breakthroughs at this point. We may experiment with this before the weekend is over."

BLIND TRUST

In the next session the members of the group are again paired, this time with new partners. The instructions are clear. You find yourself with eyes closed being led about the room with your part-

ner's hand on your wrist. He places your hand on a smooth, round
object. What could it be? You hadn't remembered anything in the
room with that shape or texture. Next you find your hand on the
rough texture of the drapes, then against the cool glass of the win-
dow pane. You become aware of the various sensations of rough-
ness and of temperature.

A few moments later, your partner leads you across the room
briskly. At first you hold back, fearing that you will bump into
something, but gradually you relax and move at your partner's
touch. He stops you and places your hand on someone's shoulder.
Your hand explores the texture of the jacket, the strength of the
shoulder itself, the muscular arm. You move on, and suddenly it
is time to stop and reverse partners. A few minutes later and you
are with your group of twelve discussing the experience of leading
and being led.

Some members of the circle comment on the element of trust.
Tom had been able to trust Betty more than Betty could trust
Tom. Some responded to the issue of control. Bill had kept a very
firm control on Paul's wrist and permitted him no freedom to explore the objects he touched, while others had been much more
permissive. The group spends some time talking about Paul's resentment at being controlled so tightly and wonders if Bill's controlling tendency also extends to his behavior in other situations.
He admits that it may be a problem for him in his work as well.
Again you are struck by the variety of ways in which individuals
respond to the same situations.

In the afternoon you are exposed to another approach to nonverbal communication. You meet with your group of twelve in a
room with a large table. You are handed a big sheet of paper.
Crayons are on the table. You are given fifteen minutes to portray
on the paper, with colors and shapes, the answer to a question:
"How do you see yourself as a leader?" Your immediate reaction
is one of protest, if not panic.

"But I'm no artist! I couldn't pass second grade art right now."
You are reassured that artistic talent is not a requirement for the
exercise, and you are urged to go ahead and complete the assignment. You look around and notice that some members of the
group are already making huge, sweeping marks on their papers.

You decide to act like you know what you are doing, and you begin your drawing.

At the end of the fifteen minutes all the sheets are piled in the middle of the table, and the top sheet is tacked up on an easel. For five minutes the members of the group respond to what they see in the drawing. Roy's picture is first.

"I get a feeling of real strength from his use of color, particularly the bright, bold colors."

"But where is he in the picture? I can't find him."

"I think he is the dominant color in the middle, and we are the weaker colors around the edge."

"The thing that bothers me is Roy's size in relation to the others —if that really is him in the middle. I'd feel better if we were the same size."

When the five minutes are up, Roy has an opportunity to respond for three minutes. "I appreciated your comments about the use of color. I was purposely trying to express myself more forcefully. I really hadn't thought of myself as the bright spot in the middle, though perhaps I do have too high an opinion of myself. I really thought of the middle as the product of the group, with me as one of the contributors to that product, one of many leaders."

When the group has gone around the circle and discussed each picture, the leader makes some comments on the drawing process. "As we have discovered, artistic talent is not a prerequisite for this exercise. Our drawing has validity simply because it expresses us: who we are and how we feel about ourselves. And did you notice that some of us who are less skilled with words can really communicate through art? Mary really came through to me this afternoon. Up until now, Mary has said very little and I didn't feel I knew her as well as some of the others. Now I really know her."

John makes another point. "I was struck by the ways in which this technique could be adapted for use in other groups. I'm going to ask my discussion group leaders to draw themselves as group leaders. I could see using this technique with church-school teachers, a group of ministers. . . ."

RESPONDING TO MUSIC

For our next session we find ourselves in a large room with a phonograph. A lithe young woman is in charge. "We are simply going to respond to music," she announces. Your heart sinks, for a dancer you are *not*. "Don't be concerned if you don't feel you can dance. That is not important. The important thing is to relax and let your body respond to the music in any way it wants to." You find yourself sweating. You wonder how you might make good your escape. Too late. The music has begun, soft trembling music. You are seated on the rug. The instructor suggests that you begin by responding with your hands. Soon you are moving your arms to the rhythm, then your head, and finally your torso. You sit and talk with your partner about how you feel in response to the music, what the music says to you, how you felt self-conscious at first. By the end of the session you are on your feet, moving rhythmically around the room to a wild Greek dance, surprised at your feeling of freedom and exhilaration. "When we feel more free to let our bodies respond to beauty, to music, to people, we are more joyful persons," says the young woman.

Early the next morning the group gathers for a brief worship period. You are asked to lie down flat on your back on the floor, with sufficient space between persons so that you do not bother each other. The leader then suggests that you tense every muscle in your body as tightly as you can. Then you consciously try to relax the body until you are lying very still, breathing quietly but deeply. The group is in silence for several minutes. You find yourself relaxing into the silence, feeling its refreshment, its healing. The leader reads a very brief statement about the power silence holds for us *if* we are open to it, and then you experience silence again for fifteen minutes. Suddenly the time is up, and you are astounded. Silence had always been such a burden before, and you were sure there must be another ten minutes left. You are disappointed that the time is gone.

As the conferees discuss their response to the experience during the coffee break, you realize that there is great potential in the proper use of silence. Pete makes one point: "I realize now that

I had always been fighting the silence. This time the physical relaxation helped me to forget about my body and just be open to it."

"I don't understand it," Rita adds, "but I felt closer to God or the divine or whatever you want to call it than I ever have. It was a feeling of joy or exaltation or something. I think being with this group also had something to do with it, but I'm not sure what."

Others found it less meaningful, but you determine to do some experimenting with the relationship between physical relaxation and meditation or worship. It occurs to you at that moment that there may be a tie here with yoga meditation and perhaps with some forms of Buddhism, and you vow to explore them further some day.

In the closing session, the leader is discussing experimental group methods. "The key to this frontier is variety of approaches. While talking is meaningful for some, another approach must be found to reach others. Some of you really emerged as persons in the drawing session, others blossomed during the movement to music session. For too long a time we have limited ourselves to one approach and simply stifled a lot of wonderful people who might have been turned on by some other method. What is good for the goose may not interest the gander, and we now know better than to stay in the same old rut week after week."

THE MARATHON GROUP

Mary has a question. "What about these marathon groups we read about? What do you think of them?"

The reply is careful, measured. "Marathon group experiences are a recent invention, and they have great value in some situations. In a marathon, the group meets for twenty-four hours or even thirty or thirty-six hours without taking a break. You stay in the same room without leaving except for necessary personal reasons. Even the meals are brought into the room. This way the continuity of the group is unbroken. If a group meets once a week for two hours, in twelve weeks it will have accumulated twenty-four hours of work. In between meetings, however, a great deal is going on to water down the group experience. In a marathon, you not only have twenty-four hours of work, but the cumulative effect is tremendous. In addition, in a marathon you begin knowing that a good share of the group's time belongs to you, and you may feel free to share a deep concern because you know there is time to work it through. As a result, the group tends to begin with a deep level of trust."

"Don't people get tired?" asks Grady. "I'm worn out after a one-hour staff meeting."

"No," is the reply. "It is amazing how little sleep is required when we are deeply and personally involved with other people. If someone simply can't keep his eyes open, he is allowed to doze if he wishes. He may simply be avoiding something, too, and the group has the right to push him if they feel that is the case."

You are skeptical, so you ask, "Is this something you suggest we try in a church?"

"Certainly not," is the leader's immediate answer. "A marathon group experience requires skilled leadership and is a specialized tool that the average person should not attempt to use. As we develop more skilled leadership, the marathon may prove to be a great instrument of growth and learning in some settings, but it should be used with care. It simply underscores the power and potential of a small group for health-giving and growth under the proper conditions. I recommend that you attend a marathon yourselves some time, but do not try to lead one without the proper training."

The leader goes on to say that many of the new group methods fall into the same category. They are highly useful in the hands of a skilled leader, but should be used with caution. He does point out that many of the simple encounter exercises used during the weekend are useful and could be used in a variety of church settings to great advantage.

The conference leader stands. The time is up, the conference ended. "We'll try one more new method before you go," he says smiling. "This is known as a group hug." Members of the group crowd together as closely as they can, until everyone is packed into a small space. It is a very pleasant experience simply to feel the nearness, the warmth, the friendship and affection of these people with whom you have shared some significant moments. You leave with a little tightness in your throat.

You pack your bag and start for your car determined to be more adventurous in experimenting with new methods of relationship. You have experienced a deeper fellowship in two days than you had imagined possible, and you are determined to share this good news with others.

POSTSCRIPT: THE FINE ART
OF SQUELCHING A SMALL GROUP

The ability to squelch the life out of a small group may be thought of as an art. Because of the strong interest in this new art, the following ground rules are offered to give direction and purpose to would-be squelchers who wish to develop their talents in this direction.

I. Dominate the group from the beginning. Establish yourself as the authority on all matters that may come before the group. Make all the basic decisions yourself, while giving the impression of a democratic spirit to the group members.

II. Pay no attention to the needs and interests of the group members. Most people don't know what is best for them anyhow.

III. Keep the discussion on a theoretical plane, preferably in the realm of theology and philosophy. Mention names like Kant, Schleiermacher, and Tillich occasionally to make the others feel inferior.

IV. If possible, establish yourself as the teacher of the group and deliver a learned lecture at each meeting. (Our rock-bound guarantee: the group won't last more than three months this way or your money back!)

V. Don't permit the fiction to arise that group members should take turns leading the discussion. They're liable to get too deeply involved and interested and keep the group alive in spite of your efforts.

VI. Never allow group members to share anything personal. Change the subject to a nice safe intellectual discussion when this happens. That way they won't get too involved with each other at a depth level. Groups in which this happens become devilishly hard to squelch.

VII. By all means, don't encourage all members of the group to express themselves. Limit the participation to the more vocal, intellectual members to keep the conversation on a high plane of sophistication. They will bore each other to sleep.

VIII. Don't urge the silent members of the group to speak up. They might get the idea that you really care about them and that their ideas count after all. They will be more difficult to discourage as a result.

IX. Allow one or two persons to dominate the discussion. That way the others will become quietly angry and the group will fold up in no time. By all means, don't point out to the dominators what they are doing. This might lead to some hurt feelings and personal growth—things to be avoided at all costs in squelching a group.

X. Keep the small group too large for the members to really get to know each other. By all means have at least twenty or twenty-five members in order to do this.

XI. Include a long business meeting with each group session and bore everyone to tears. The group will rapidly wither.

XII. Arrange the seats in formal rows like a classroom. Don't permit informality to sneak in by sitting in a friendly circle. In that situation group members might feel encouraged to express themselves and not want to give up the group.

XIII. Answer all questions yourself. Don't let group members speak to each other or answer each other's questions. What do they know that you can't say better?

XIV. By all means don't let group members express any hostility they may feel toward each other. You may find them understanding each other too well as a result and the group will become tenacious of continuing.

XV. Complain at every meeting about how few people have

turned out. This will give group members a size-consciousness and sense of guilt. They will either quit coming or they will invite their friends and the small group will soon grow into oblivion; it will become a large group.

NOTE: It is recommended that every group leader express his own unique personality in using the above rules. There is a squelching method that is uniquely yours. You may have found ways to squelch a group that haven't even been thought of yet. But follow any one of these rules with dogged persistence and you need not fear. You will have expressed yourself. The group will certainly collapse, for you will have violated a principle of human nature.[1]

[1] Adapted from an article by the author in *The Laymen's Movement Review*, Vol. VII, No. 3 (1964).

SOME SUGGESTIONS
FOR FURTHER READING

SMALL GROUPS IN THE CHURCH

ANDERSON, PHILIP A. *Church Meetings That Matter*. Philadelphia–Boston: United Church Press, 1965. Paperback.

CASTEEL, JOHN L. (ed.). *Spiritual Renewal Through Personal Groups*. New York: Association Press, 1957.

——— (ed.). *The Creative Role of Interpersonal Groups in the Church Today*. New York: Association Press, 1968.

DESHLER, G. BYRON. *The Power of the Personal Group*. Nashville, Tenn.: Tidings.

Groups That Work. Grand Rapids, Mich.: Zondervan, 1967.

LESLIE, ROBERT C. (ed.). Special issue on "Small Groups in the Church," *Pastoral Psychology* (June, 1964).

LITTLE, SARA. *Learning Together in the Christian Fellowship*. Richmond, Va.: John Knox Press, 1960.

MITCHELL, KENNETH R. *Psychological and Theological Relationships in the Multiple Staff Ministry*. Philadelphia: Westminster Press, 1966.

RAINES, ROBERT A. *New Life in the Church*. New York: Harper & Row, 1961.

REID, CLYDE H. "Small Group Insights for the Servant Ministry," *Pastoral Psychology* (April, 1968).

——— (ed.). Special issue on "Ministry Through Small Groups," *Pastoral Psychology* (March, 1967).

GENERAL WRITINGS ON SMALL GROUPS

BENNIS, WARREN G., BENNE, KENNETH D., and CHIN, ROBERT. *The Planning of Change.* New York: Holt, Rinehart & Winston, 1961.

BENNIS, WARREN G., SCHEIN, EDGAR H., BERLEW, DAVID E., and STEELE, FRED I. *Interpersonal Dynamics.* Homewood, Ill.: Dorsey Press, 1964.

HARE, PAUL, BORGATTA, EDGAR F., and BALES, ROBERT F. *Small Groups.* New York: Alfred A. Knopf, 1955.

KNOWLES, MALCOLM and HULDA. *Introduction to Group Dynamics.* New York: Association Press, 1959.

SCHEIN, EDGAR H., and BENNIS, WARREN G. *Personal and Organizational Change Through Group Methods: The Laboratory Approach.* New York–London–Sydney: John Wiley & Sons, 1965.

SCHUTZ, WILLIAM C. *Joy.* New York: Grove Press, 1967.

"Selected Reading Series." Washington, D.C.: National Training Laboratories–National Education Association, 1961. Paperback series of six.

STRAUSS, BERT and FRANCES. *New Ways to Better Meetings.* New York: Viking Press, 1957.

TRAINING OPPORTUNITIES

A variety of workshops and small group experiences are offered by the following agencies who will supply information upon request:

Associates for Human Resources
387 Sudbury Road
Concord, Massachusetts   01742

Aureon Institute
71 Park Avenue
New York, New York   10016

Boston University Human Relations Center
270 Bay State Road
Boston, Massachusetts   02215

Department of Educational Development
National Council of Churches
475 Riverside Drive, Room 714
New York, New York   10027
   (Spring workshop at Green Lake, Wisconsin)

Esalen Institute
Big Sur Hot Springs
Big Sur, California   93920

Gestalt Institute of Cleveland
12921 Euclid Avenue
Cleveland, Ohio   44112

Institute for Advanced Pastoral Studies
380 Lone Pine Road
Bloomfield Hills, Michigan   48013
   (for clergy and laity)

Kopavi, Inc.
1618 Eustis Street, Apt. 12
St. Paul, Minnesota   55108

NTL Institute for Applied Behavioral Science
1201 Sixteenth Street, N.W.
Washington, D.C.   20036
   (Summer workshops at Bethel, Maine, and elsewhere.)

Oasis
Midwest Center for Human Potential
Stone-Brandel Center
1439 S. Michigan Avenue
Chicago, Illinois   60605

DATE DUE

Jensen			
DEC 18 1985			
DEC 05 1987			
GAYLORD			PRINTED IN U.S.A.

36982